STOP DOMESTIC VIOLENCE

Innovative Skills, Techniques, Options, and Plans for Better Relationships

Also by David B. Wexler

The Adolescent Self
The PRISM Workbook
The Advanced PRISM Workbook
Domestic Violence 2000

A Norton Professional Book

STOP DOMESTIC VIOLENCE

Innovative Skills, Techniques, Options, and Plans for Better Relationships

GROUP LEADER'S MANUAL

David B. Wexler

W. W. NORTON & COMPANY
New York • London

David B. Wexler, Ph.D. is a clinical psychologist in San Diego and the Executive Director of the Relationship Training Institute (www.RTIprojects.com). He may be contacted at info@RTIprojects.com.

Please note that the exercises and handouts developed for *The STOP Program* may not be copied or reproduced in any form without written consent from the publisher.

Composition and book design by Techbooks
Manufacturing by Hamilton Printing
Production Manager: Leeann Graham

Library of Congress Cataloging-in-Publication Data

Wexler, David B.
    Stop domestic violence : innovative skills, techniques, options, and plans for
  better relationships : group leader's manual / David B. Wexler.
        p.   cm. — (Norton professional book)
    Includes bibliographical references and index.
    Contents: Pt. 1. Foundations – pt. 2. Special program sessions – pt. 3. Group sessions.
      ISBN-13: 978-0-393-70514-0
      ISBN-10: 0-393-70514-5
        1. Wife abuse—Prevention—Handbooks, manuals, etc.   2. Abusive men—
  Rehabilitation—Handbooks, manuals, etc.   3. Group psychotherapy—
  Handbooks, manuals, etc.   I. Title. II. Series.

    HV6626.W44 2006
    362.82'9254—dc22   2006045339

ISBN 13: 978-0-393-70514-0 (pbk.)
ISBN 10: 0-393-70514-5 (pbk.)

W. W. Norton & Company, Inc., 500 Fifth Avenue, New York, N.Y. 10110
www.wwnorton.com

W. W. Norton & Company Ltd., Castle House, 75/76 Wells St., London W1T 3QT

1 2 3 4 5 6 7 8 9 0

To all the men who have changed, and to all the men who will.

Contents

Acknowledgments

The original development of the *The STOP Program* treatment model for domestic violence emerged from a collaborative effort as part of a research project evaluating military domestic violence treatment programs, cosponsored by the Department of Defense and the National Institute of Mental Health. The research was conducted by a team from the University of Colorado, headed by principal investigator Franklyn W. Dunford, Ph.D., who offered sage counsel and impeccable support to the fine-tuning of this program. I would like to particularly express my gratitude to the U.S. Navy Family Advocacy Program administrators and staff throughout the years for offering so much support and invaluable creative contributions to this body of work.

Daniel G. Saunders, Ph.D., was a primary consultant and contributor to this treatment program from the outset. Some of his specific contributions are noted in the text, but many of his informal contributions are not. He has brought vast experience in the field of domestic violence and the highest standards of professionalism to our programs and this manual.

I would also like to thank the clinical consultant staff of the Relationship Training Institute, who have been providing outstanding clinical services for the Navy Family Advocacy Center in San Diego since 1986. Their contributions to the program and to the refinement of this manual have been outstanding I would particularly like to thank James A. Reavis, Psy.D., for his significant contributions. In recent years, the clinical staff has included Daniel Blaess, Ph.D., Sage De Beixidon Breslin, Ph.D., Stacy Buhbe, Ph.D., Dennis Harris, MFT, and Karen Hyland, Ph.D. Their expertise and passion for this work has contributed in immeasurable ways to the program presented here. I would also like to offer special thanks to Cynthia Martin, Ph.D. and Karen McCardle, MFT for their passion for baseball and for offering so much to the work we do.

The San Diego Domestic Violence Council, and the coordinated community efforts of city attorney, district attorney, police department, judges, community agencies, and victim support groups, have provided an extremely fertile climate for the development of these ideas.

Many thanks also to my mentors and heroes in this sacred work: Donald Dutton, Amy Holtzworth-Munroe, Jackson Katz, Don Meichenbaum, Bill O'Hanlon, John Gottman, Terry Real, Bill Pollack, Ron Levant.

Finally, thanks to all the men who have given so much of themselves and worked so hard throughout our years of treatment. We have found that men who commit acts of domestic violence come in many shapes and sizes and that each man has a unique story to tell.

Introduction

In this field, you have to stay fresh. The work is too important, and the consequences of missteps too tragic, to stand still.

Prior to the 1970s, when men were accused of domestic violence it was usually considered a "family thing." Unless it was too serious to ignore, police typically looked the other way, nobody identified the problem as a significant social issue, and no substantive programs existed to identify the problem, treat the abusers, and offer support for the victims.

Beginning in the 1970s and 1980s, with breathtaking speed and innovation, the feminist movement insisted on drawing attention to the issue of domestic violence and identified partner abuse as an issue of gender politics that required consciousness raising for men and support for women. This wave of attention led to the development of women's shelters, men's groups to challenge the attitudes and behavior of male abusers, and the development of specialized units in police departments, courts, and probation departments. At least in the more progressive states and counties, domestic violence charges were taken seriously, and programs were established to address the tragic cost of these behaviors. Male relationship violence was identified as part of a larger pattern of sexist attitudes, male entitlement, and men using aggression to get their way when they felt like it. The driving force of all male relationship violence was targeted as "power and control." Violent women were primarily identified as acting in self-defense. Programs to rehabilitate male abusers were considered to be educational in nature to "reprogram" male attitudes and expectations in relationships.

And now, with deep gratitude to those who demanded attention and rethinking of these issues, we continue to move forward. Men abuse women, but some women abuse men. We now know that one size does not fit all: only a minority of male domestic violence represents true battering, or "intimate terrorism," while the majority (both male and female) instead represents "situational couple violence." While the power and control theme still drives some of the most disturbing male abuse, many men are simply driven more by skills deficits in managing the complexities of emotionally intimate relationships.

And, most importantly for our purposes here, and for the purposes of treating those men who have abused their female partners, we now know that the best way to "rehabilitate" these men is not by branding them as "batterers" or by demanding that they identify their behavior as driven by power and control themes. The trends in the field indicate that the most effective way, simply, of treating abusers is to offer them respect as men. We must always insist on full accountability for behavior, but we need to recognize these men's own profound sense of powerlessness in relationships. And we need to help equip them with better models for making sense of relationship problems and help them develop a wider range of emotionally intelligent skills for responding to them. At times, we need to honor their perspective that their female partners often engage in violent behavior that is not strictly self-defense. We need to equip them with tools for handling relationship conflicts more successfully—based on the assumption that this is what most men actually want, rather than assuming the opposite.

And in so doing, we aim to accomplish our mission of helping these men become the best men they can be, and to reduce—ideally, to eliminate—the likelihood of relationship violence in the future. This is the mission of *The STOP Program*, the manual for which, *STOP Domestic Violence: Innovative Skills, Techniques, Options, and Plans for Better Relationships*, is improved, upgraded, and newly informed by the flood of research and new models in this field. Those professionals who are already familiar with the *Domestic Violence 2000* program will recognize many familiar themes as well as many new ones.

PART I
FOUNDATIONS

PROGRAM NOTES

The STOP Program is the new, improved, and updated version of the *Domestic Violence 2000* program published in 1999. Like the original, *The STOP Program* integrates elements from feminist, cognitive–behavioral, and self psychological models for treating domestic violence. The program format and message insist that men examine the dominance and control aspects of domestic violence—especially issues of male entitlement and privilege. It offers men intensive training in new skills for self-management, communication, problem solving, and empathy for others. And group counselors consistently employ a client-centered approach that emphasizes respect for the men's experience—both in personal history and in present relationships—and empathic understanding of why men choose to act the way they do. The approach is political, educational, and psychological. This model had been carefully constructed through almost 20 years of trial-and-error and by paying attention to input from new research in the field.

Now there is so much more that we know about how domestic violence takes place and about what works in treating it, and *The STOP Program* integrates this new information.

1. **Program Design:** This manual is designed for use in an open-ended 26-week or 52-week psychoeducational treatment program for male domestic violence offenders. (Because the program is organized in an open-ended fashion, with group members often starting at different points in the program, the midpoint and exit sessions are not presented in situ.) For a 52-week group program, simply start the cycle over when the 26 sessions are completed. Although some group members will repeat the content, they will still benefit from reviewing the material again. In fact, many of the content themes are reviewed repeatedly anyway throughout the 26 sessions because this contributes to overall integration. Nobody in a domestic violence program has ever suffered from learning the same information twice.

2. **Session Structure:** Each session is designed for a two-hour period, with a 10-minute break in the middle. Also, please note that all group sessions begin with a brief review of the "Weekly Check-in" (see "Standard Forms" section), which the group members must fill out prior to the beginning of each group session. The group leaders should briefly review the completed check-in forms to alert them to any specific issues to be covered in that session. Group size should be at least three members, and no more than twelve. Eight group members is ideal.

3. **Handouts:** The group members in this program use *The Stop Program: Handouts and Homework*, which includes all of the forms, exercises, and homework assignments for the 26 sessions and the additional material. Note that the *Handouts and Homework* materials also appear in the group leader's manual, indicated by a star at the top of the page. The forms are three-hole punched for use in a personal binder. Individual programs can be created by adding or subtracting some of these materials.

4. **Teaching Methods:** These sessions are designed to be psychoeducational, with lecture, demonstration, and role-playing, as well as personal group discussion. Both the educational and the psychological are essential for the program's success. In order for group members to properly learn the skills and techniques, group discussion of personal experiences and specific applications is encouraged.

5. **Evaluation Form:** At regular intervals throughout this program (approximately every 5 to 10 sessions), review with group members the "Evaluation Form" (see "Standard Forms" section) that you will be using to evaluate each member's performance. Explain each of the criteria. Although you should review this during their initial orientation, make it clear that we repeat it so they will be fully informed about what we value and look for in this program. As you review each item, ask at least one group member to assess his own performance in this area. This is an excellent opportunity to offer genuine feedback, bolster self-esteem, and stimulate increased mutual support from group members.

6. **Homework:** Homework is regularly assigned throughout these sessions. The previous session's homework should be reviewed at the beginning of each session; the next session's homework assigned at the end. It is not necessary (and too time-consuming) to carefully review each group member's homework each session. However, it is essential to at least review one or two examples of the homework and to conduct a quick visual check to make sure all group members have completed the work. Group members will quickly recognize if homework is not taken seriously and thus, they will not take it seriously.

7. **Orientation Sessions (prior to each monthly new member session):** Several forms are included for meeting with new group members in the hour prior to their first group session. Research has indicated that this pregroup preparation is extremely valuable in setting the stage for successful treatment. **It is highly recommended that new members only be allowed into the groups one week out of the month so that the remaining sessions each month are not disrupted by new admissions.**

8. **New Member Sessions:** When new members are entering the group, *The STOP Program* model is to engage in a brief "getting to know you" exercise (described in the new member sessions information) and to review one of two exercises with the group: "House of Abuse" or "Time-Out." If the "House of Abuse" is reviewed in the January new member session, "Time-Out" will be reviewed in February, and so on. This information is so central to our work that it bears repeating for the veteran group members, who actually "get it" better and better with every repetition.

   The material in the new member sessions is not a replacement for the scheduled material in the 26 sessions. It should be integrated into the overall format of those sessions as much as possible.

9. **Midpoint Sessions:** The "Switch!" exercise is designed as a kind of "midterm exam" for group members. Group members will be, at any given time, at very different points in their treatment completion, so this exercise should be introduced when an individual group member is approximately halfway through his program. In other words, if you are running a 26-week program, he will do this exercise at his own 13th session.

   The material of the midpoint session is not a replacement for the scheduled material in the 26 sessions. It should be integrated into the overall format of that session as much as possible.

10. **Exit Sessions:** When an individual group member is within three sessions of completing his program, he should go through the first "Exit" exercise ("Most Violent or Most Disturbing Incident"). At his final session, he should review his "Prevention Plan." All group members will thus have witnessed a number of these successful "graduations" by the time their turn comes.

    The material in the exit sessions is not a replacement for the scheduled material in the 26 sessions. It should be integrated into the overall format of that session as much as possible.

11. **Standard Forms:** Several standard forms are included for use in the programs. Each form may be used as is, adapted for the needs of the particular program, or abandoned completely. The key forms are:

    - Evaluation Form
    - Weekly Check-in
    - What Is Most Helpful?
    - Gut Check Questionnaire

    "What Is Most Helpful?" and "The Gut Check Questionnaire" are both very valuable handouts to help generate discussion about group process and individual progress. They are not designed to be used with any particular session but it is recommended that group leaders use these whenever they feel that these discussions would be valuable.

12. **The Nine Commandments:** "The Nine Commandments" handout on page 36 contains the central themes that run through all the treatment sessions, even if there are no specific lectures devoted to them. A poster-size version of these commandments should be placed on the group room wall. Whenever a subject related to any of the commandments emerges in the group discussion, it is helpful to interrupt, point to the poster, and ask someone to read aloud the relevant commandment. "The Nine Commandments" are carefully reviewed in the initial orientation session.

13. **Male and Female Cofacilitators:** The optimal format for leading the groups involves a male and female cofacilitator team. The group members benefit from a counseling relationship with therapists of both genders. We have generally found it valuable for the *male* coleader to take the lead when confronting any group members regarding female bashing or negative generalizations about women. This models a different male consciousness about male–female politics— which sounds different when a female appears to be merely defending herself or her gender. The best model, from our experience, is for the male group leader to send the message that even men can be offended by sexism. The cofacilitator team can also effectively model respectful disagreement and conflict resolution.

Please do not take this as a criticism of programs that run groups with single group leaders or with two men or even two women. These can all work well. However, if funding, resources, and personnel allow, then *The STOP Program* design is most optimal with a male–female team.

14. **Treatment Failure (see "Provisional Status Policy"):** If any group member is showing clear signs that treatment is not progressing successfully, he should be confronted about his behavior and informed as early as possible in the treatment program that there is a problem. We usually expect to be able to flag these problems by week 6 or 7. It is unfair to inform a group member after 23 sessions that we have decided he is not benefiting from the program (unless some unexpected event, like a reabuse, has suddenly taken place). Indications of treatment failure include belligerent attitudes, refusal to do any homework, refusal to participate, or consistent verbal aggression when discussing females.

15. **Program Limitations:** When introducing new skills, such as assertiveness, to the group members, it is very important to emphasize that there is no guarantee that these skills will always bring about a positive outcome. In fact, there are times when being "assertive" or using "active listening" or "I" messages is not the best course. The message we should send is that usually these are the most *respectful* forms of communication, and *respectful* communication is generally the most effective in the long run.

16. *The STOP Program* **Limitations:** Many aspects of conducting a comprehensive domestic violence treatment program are *not* included in this manual: supporting victims, intake and assessment procedures, dealing with fee arrangements, coordinating efforts with court systems and other agencies, or selecting and supervising staff members. *We strongly recommend that agencies develop thorough systems and policies for the wider range of services in treating domestic violence offenders.* This manual is designed only to treat heterosexual men who have committed some form of psychological or physical act or acts of abuse against their partners. However, the manual has been easily adapted for use with female perpetrators, gay and lesbian perpetrators, adolescent perpetrators, and other populations.

17. **Videotapes and Audiotapes:** Several different videos are used in many of the sessions:

    - *The Great Santini* is available for purchase from many video outlets.
        - Scene I (high school basketball game; begin at 1:03:22 and end at 1:12:18)
        - Scene II (father-son one-on-one basketball game; begin at 31:48 and end at 40:23)
        - Scene III (father/mother expressing feelings; begin at 48:23 and end at 54:05)
        - Scene IV (kids witnessing spouse abuse; begin at 1:28:29 and end at 1:29:57)
    - *Men's Work* is available from the Hazelden Foundation (1-800-328-9000).
        - Scene I (series of put-downs and masculinity challenges; begin at 2:07 and end at 11:57)
        - Scene II (spouse abuse over dinner/intervention from neighbor; begin at 19:16 and end at 23:42)

- *Affliction* is available for purchase from many video outlets.
  - The "Halloween" scene begins at 13:20 and ends at 19:25
- *Good Will Hunting* is available for purchase from many video outlets.
  - The "shame" scene begins at 1:30:23 and ends at 1:34:52

The exact timing of the specific video clips may be slightly different on different video cassette recorders.

Programs are strongly encouraged to use their own video clips to specifically illustrate key points in this program. However, only brief video clips should be used—group members should never be stuck in a room to watch a one- or two-hour video. This is not the best use of group time.

The relaxation CD-ROM, containing *Quieting Reflex* and the *Brief Quieting Reflex*, is included in your book purchase. Similar relaxation tapes or exercises may be substituted.

RULES OF ENGAGEMENT

Assumptions

1. All of us working in the field of domestic violence treatment and prevention recognize that we have one primary mission: to reduce the likelihood—ideally, to eliminate—the risk of future relationship violence.

2. Programs like *The STOP Program* are committed to targeting the men who have been identified as perpetrators of relationship violence, and doing everything possible to positively impact how they conduct themselves in the future. Our goal is one of rehabilitation and change.

3. In working with men who have committed these acts of relationship violence, our most effective strategy is to "engage" the group member to increase the likelihood that he will be receptive to change. If we don't reach them, we can't change them.

Communicating Respect

It is often difficult for group leaders to listen dispassionately and compassionately to the stories of the men in our program. We all enter this setting with our own values and judgments—let alone personal experiences—and the process of understanding a man who abuses his partner can provoke difficult emotions.

The men in this program deserve our respect—not, obviously, for the actions they have taken, but rather for the individual stories that have led them to act in desperate and destructive ways. It is very helpful to recognize that many of the men in our groups, like all of us, have become overwhelmed by emotions, and lacked the necessary range of skills to handle those emotions in constructive and proactive ways. Although we must always emphasize personal responsibility, it is also essential to recognize our essential similarity and their essential humanity.

It is our belief that when these men become smarter about themselves (more aware of needs, feelings, and motivations) and smarter about their options (better skills at self-talk, relaxation, communication, empathy, and problem solving), they will choose to behave in more appropriate ways.

Pacing and leading (see "Pacing and Leading" guidelines on page 18): One treatment strategy to help facilitate these goals is called "pacing and leading." This approach employs the process of carefully *mirroring*—or *pacing*—the experience of the other person, followed by a *leading* suggestion for a new way to think or act.

This sequence of communicating empathic understanding and respect for the man's experience, followed by a new perspective or idea, proves very valuable in these groups.

Labeling: It is vital to communicate this message: *We treat the man, not the label.* Stay away from labels that sound like put-downs, such as *batterers, perpetrators,* or *abusers.* Those labels may be correct, and they may be the labels used in the legal system, but they do nothing but foster shame and resistance in these groups. We want the men to understand that we could put any man in this group, regardless of what has gone wrong in his relationship patterns, and he would benefit from the approaches used in this treatment model.

Reframing negative emotions: It is both respectful and productive to reframe negative emotions such as jealousy, hurt, and feeling disrespected as signs of attachment: "*If you didn't care about her, and what she thinks of you, this wouldn't matter so much.*" Of course, this cannot be the only perspective on these emotions, but they do allow the men to examine these emotions without automatically coming to extreme negative conclusions about themselves, their partner, or their relationship. It is also valuable to help them apply this same perspective to the negative emotional states of their partners.

Initial resistance: Very frequently group members enter the first group session angry and resistant. They complain about being in the group, challenge the group policies, and insist that they will not be talking in these sessions. Unless they are seriously disruptive to the group, it is usually best to respectfully listen to their complaints and then move on. *Power struggles should be avoided whenever possible.* Often men who are the most difficult in the early sessions turn out to be the best group members, so long as they have felt respected.

Taking things seriously: Often, the group members will become uncomfortable with the emotionally disturbing discussions that emerge in the group, and they deal with this by laughing or making fun. Sometimes this happens when a group member describes some act of violence toward his wife or partner that he committed because she was nagging him so much. It can get tiring for the group leaders to "lecture" the group about how "this is not a funny subject." Often, modeling has the most impact. The group leaders should simply maintain a serious tone themselves. The group members usually get the message quickly. Many of these men are surprisingly sensitive to social cues about correct behavior and they don't want to "look bad."

System bashing: System bashing also occurs frequently in the groups, such as bashing the court system, child protective services, or child custody laws. These discussions should be short-circuited as quickly as possible. Unlike women bashing, however, it is rarely effective to confront these complaints. For one thing, the men may be justified in their complaints. For another, it is unproductive to engage in any unnecessary power struggles. The most effective strategy is to say something like this: "*You know, you may be right about some of your complaints, but this isn't really the focus of the group sessions. What we need to talk about here is the things you can do differently in your lives.*"

Women bashing: Women bashing often occurs in these group sessions. In contrast to system bashing, this should be confronted *immediately.* Group leaders should point out that generalizations about any social group always turn people into categories rather than individuals. It should be emphasized that "*It's OK to say that your wife complains a lot, but not to say that all women are nags.*" Furthermore, men who refer to their wife as "the wife" or "she" or even "my wife" should be consistently asked to refer to her *by name*. It can be "humanizing" to write the name of each of the "women" in the group on the board as their names come up during each session. Our goal is to make the women in these men's lives as real and human as possible.

Powerlessness and accountability: Although it is obvious that dominance and control are central themes for many of the male domestic violence perpetrators, it is also important to recognize how *powerless* many of these men feel. When we can identify this experience of powerlessness, many of these men are much more accessible to us. They feel less blamed as bad people and more understood as men who have been frustrated or have felt wounded. It is quite possible to communicate this message without absolving men of responsibility for their abusive actions. Consider this message: "*We want you to take 100% of the responsibility for your own behavior, but not necessarily 100% of the blame for all the problems.*"

A User-friendly Environment

Not only is it important to engage the group members by communicating respect, but this atmosphere of respect is also communicated through the structure of the program and the treatment environment that we design for them. It is also important to recognize the learning styles of the men in our groups and design interventions accordingly.

Shame-free group names: Domestic violence treatment groups should not be called domestic violence treatment groups, at least not so far as the group members are concerned. The names should be neutral, like *Group HAWK* or *Group EAGLE*, or positive, like *Relationship Skills Training* or *The STOP Program*. These men are very sensitive to being and feeling shamed about their behavior, and the shame experience rarely makes them more amenable to change. Instead, it generates defensiveness and resistance.

"Shame-friendly" group environment: The discussion in the group should not lead to more shaming than they are already experiencing. It is one thing to challenge the group members to recognize the ways in which their behavior has been abusive; communicating disgust is another. There needs to be room for them to discuss their feelings of shame about their behavior without feeling more of it. The goal is to create a shame-friendly group environment in which shame can be identified and integrated.

Interactive, engaging techniques: Another important design issue for these programs is to make sure that the information that is so vital for their progress is presented in ways that are engaging and user friendly. Lectures need to be simple and straightforward. The use of video clips, group exercises, demonstrations, role-plays, and humor all enhance the attention span and receptivity of our audience.

Offering couples treatment options: Many state statutes prohibit any couples treatment options, at least until the offender has fully completed his or her own treatment program. In many cases, this policy make sense. However, many of the men in our programs know that their partner has also significantly contributed to the violence at home. Even if it is not used in a particular case, the awareness among group members that couples' treatment is available communicates the message that the program understands the complexity of many domestic violence situations.

Subculture-specific groups: Again, this may not be possible at all sites and many programs may object to this on theoretical grounds. However, sometimes men of various subcultures or minority groups (African American, Mexican American,

Filipino, and certainly gay) feel more comfortable and can be more open in these homogenous groups.

Therapeutic Alliance

Another obvious issue in generating the engagement experience revolves around specific interventions to foster a therapeutic alliance. Years of research about the efficacy of clinical interventions in any setting have taught us that this variable is one of the most essential contributors to any treatment success.

Often this alliance is generated naturally, if the counselors have an intuitive sense of how to foster an alliance and if the group member is receptive. Most professionals working in this field are already skilled at this. The brief list of ideas below are intended as reminders of some specific approaches that may enhance this alliance even further.

Group leader self-disclosure: Therapist self-disclosure, in moderation, can be very effective in these groups. Group leaders have often created an atmosphere of increased trust and intimacy by acknowledging that some of the same struggles and conflicts have taken place in their own relationships. This is a very valuable tool in helping group members normalize their experiences, and often enables them to react less explosively to family and personal frustrations.

Although it is difficult to establish an absolute set of rules of when or when not to self-disclose, it may be assumed that group leader self-disclosure is contraindicated in the following situations:

Revealing the "too personal": It is important not to reveal information that might place a burden on group members to take care of the counselor, or that might lead to a loss of professional credibility if others in the field became aware of this same information.

Needing a friend: The reason to self-disclose is to offer something to help the group. If a professional finds him- or herself talking about a recent divorce because the professional needs to talk to someone about it and the people in the group are very interested, this is a mistake.

Needing admiration: Sometimes people in the counseling field, if they are not careful, use their clients to feel admired for personal accomplishments (famous people they may know, a book than have published, an important position for which they have been chosen). It is not the job of the group to provide admiration.

Losing credibility: If revealing personal information may actually lead to the loss of credibility with the group members, then this would be a mistake. A woman who had been in an abusive relationship, and revealed this to the group with the intention of telling them that she knew a lot about this area, would find members suspecting that she would be unable to see them clearly as individual men. If the group leader has served in the military, or if he or she has been happily married for 25 years, revealing this information may increase credibility about relationships—or it may signal to the men that the group leader can't relate to them or doesn't know enough about tormented relationships.

Normalizing violence: If a group member reports a violent urge or fantasy when arguing with his wife, it is not appropriate for the leader to tell the group that he or she often feels the same way. Even if it is true, this tends to normalize aggressive impulses. The group members get the message that everyone feels as they do, which is not exactly true. Everyone has anger, and perhaps even occasional aggressive urges, but most people do not seriously struggle with whether or not to act on them—as these men have.

Universal experience: It is very valuable for group members to hear the basic message that "Anybody could benefit from this program." In other words, these men are not criminal freaks. They are men who, like all of us, have failed sometimes in handling the complexities of love relationships. Without in any way minimizing the seriousness and tragedy of their offenses, it is still very treatment friendly to make it clear that the group leaders, too, could benefit from going through a program like this which examines relationship assumptions and relationship behavior.

Pregroup preparation: As Yalom (1995) has indicated, one of the most valuable contributors to the success of "brief" group therapies is the use of appropriate pregroup preparation. This helps right off the bat to foster the alliance necessary for successful group performance. The orientation session of *The STOP Program,* which usually involves a single or very small group meeting privately with the group leaders, is designed with exactly these principles in mind. We want to have the new, unsure, and defensive group member form an alliance with the group leader(s) without the competition of the rest of the group.

TYPOLOGIES OF DOMESTIC VIOLENCE OFFENDERS
One Size Does Not Fit All

"Who are these guys?"

Recent research in the field of determining different types of domestic violence offenders has yielded valuable insights into how and why domestic violence takes place. The research has been conducted almost exclusively on adult male heterosexual offenders and should not automatically be applied to domestic violence offenders who are adolescent, female, or gay. We know now that the men who commit these acts have a wide variety of motivations, triggers for aggression, personal histories, and personality styles, and they operate in a variety of relationships.

This is not intended to be a comprehensive review of the research and theory in this field. In the years of developing *The STOP Program,* we have particularly found the research of Dr. Amy Holtzworth-Munroe (Holtzworth-Munroe & Stuart, 1994, Holtzworth-Munroe, Meehan, Herron, Rehman, & Stuart, 2000), at Indiana University, to be valuable. This research and other contributions will be reviewed here.

Similarities

While we now know how varied domestic violence offenders are, it is also important to first summarize the factors that they (adult, male, heterosexual, domestic violence offenders) have in common. Here's what the research tells us:

As compared to nonoffenders:

- They hold attitudes that evaluate the use of force less negatively.
- They distort the causes and consequences of their behavior.
- They assume greater negative intent on the part of their partners.
- They are less able to use reasoning.
- They have higher levels of arousal in response to conflict.
- They have higher generalized anger/hostility.
- They label many forms of negative affect (hurt, jealousy, fear) as anger.

Typologies and Differences

Holtzworth-Munroe, Meehan et al. (2000) identified four types of male domestic violence offenders. The categories are based on assessment of frequency, severity, and generalization of violence, as well as key personality variables (such as antisocial traits, anger, depression, anxiety, jealousy, and fear of abandonment).

GENERALLY VIOLENT AGGRESSOR (GVA)

GVA offenders have early experiences which increase the risk of developing positive attitudes toward violence and negative attitudes toward women, while failing to develop social skills in intimate or nonintimate situations. Their relationship violence is simply a part of their general pattern of violent and criminal behavior. As compared to other domestic violence offenders they:

- are generally antisocial and more likely to engage in instrumental violence;
- are tend to be violent across situations and across different victims;
- are more generally belligerent;
- are more likely to abuse substances;
- are more likely to have a criminal history;
- are more likely to have been a victim of child abuse;
- are more likely to have witnessed parental spouse abuse;
- are show little remorse;
- are limited in their capacity for empathy and attachment;
- have extremely negative attitudes toward women and conservative views of relationships;
- show a high pattern of inflicting psychological and sexual abuse;
- show a high association historically with deviant peers; and
  have attitudes that are supportive of violence.

Items on the *Millon Clinical Multiaxial Inventory—III,* which contribute to this category, include the following (Millon, Millon, Davis, & Grossman; 2006, pp. 2–4):

- *I got in trouble as a teenager*
- *I have used illegal drugs*
- *I have done impulsive things that have gotten me in trouble*
- *Punishment doesn't stop me from getting in trouble*

FAMILY-ONLY (FO)

In FO offenders, the use of physical aggression emerges as a result of poor partner-specific communication skills, dependence on and preoccupation with the partner, and mild problems with impulsivity. Compared to other domstic violence offenders these men demonstrate:

- little or no significant evidence of psychopathology;
- mild social skills deficits;
- moderate dependence and jealousy;
- passive and passive–aggressive style;
- overcontrolled hostility: tendency to suppress emotions and withdraw, later erupting into violence after long periods of unexpressed but seething rage;
- generally less severe acts of abuse;
- remorse about their actions;
- reduced likelihood of being violent outside the home;
- little psychological abuse;

- liberal attitudes toward women (compared to other types of domestic violence offenders);
- low levels of anger, depression, and jealousy, but high levels of "impression management";
- reduced likelihood of having been abused as children.

LOW LEVEL ANTISOCIAL (LLA)

Low level antisocial is the category generated by the research on men whose characteristics overlapped the GVA and FO categories. They do not reach the full criteria levels for GVA, but they have enough GVA characteristics so they cannot be appropriately classified in the FO group. This category does not have a set of descriptive criteria independent of the two categories above.

BORDERLINE/DYSPHORIC (BD)

Emotionally dysphoric/borderline domestic violence offenders, when confronted with relationship conflicts, typically perceive them as threats of abandonment. Lacking the skills to resolve such conflicts, they impulsively use physical aggression to express their distress and intense anger. Compared to other domestic violence offender, these men demonstrate:

- high scores for psychopathology, impulsivity, and aggression;
- a history of parental rejection and child abuse;
- emotional volatility;
- violent tendency only within their family;
- more social isolation and social incompetence than other batterers;
- the highest levels of anger, depression, jealousy, and fear of abandonment;
- tendency to misinterpret their partners and blame their partners for their own mood states;
- prominent depression and feelings of inadequacy;
- a history of severe child abuse.

Items on the *Millon Clinical Multiaxial Inventory—III,* which contribute to this category, include the following (Millon, Millon, Davis, & Grossman, 2006, pp. 2–4):

- *I create situations where I feel hurt or rejected*
- *I will do something desperate to prevent abandonment*
- *Being alone frightens me*
- *Most people think poorly of me*

THE CONTEXT OF COMPETENCE

Generating the context of competence is an approach based on principles for solution-focused therapies (O'Hanlon & Weiner-Davis, 1989). Based on the original work of Milton Erickson, these solution-focused approaches insist on emphasizing the inherent strengths in the individual or in the family system, rather than focusing exclusively on the deficits, problems, or failures. The philosophy of the context of competence is to "catch yourself doing something right." Even when individuals have made mistakes or behaved destructively in their relationships, it is still very valuable to identify the parts that went right and build on those strengths.

This is a problem-solving approach to difficulties, which concentrates more on finding effective ways to meet challenges rather than analyzing all the reasons why someone finds himself in these difficulties (the analysis can be very interesting, but generally does not bring about change). It can be applied to a wide range of problems and challenges, and it is not limited to any one theoretical approach.

Even if a professional has never used any of the specific techniques or strategies of solution-focused therapies in a group program, it is extremely valuable in order to help create the context of competence atmosphere. Many of the men in our domestic violence programs experience intense levels of shame and failure. This not an excuse for abuse, it is just a psychological reality. If our dominant goal is to prevent future relationship violence, then one of our most valuable strategies is to help bring out their best qualities, using whatever it takes to help them get there.

Essentially, we are sending the men the message that we believe they are fully capable of handling their relationships more successfully. We want to identify those successes very clearly and reward them for doing things right, while never, of course, minimizing or ignoring doing things wrong.

Even the very first question on the "Weekly Check-in" about reporting weekly successes is a direct reflection of the context of competence orientation. In analyzing a relationship problem, it is also very helpful to identify the strengths that already exist.

Past success: "*What have we done in the past that was successful?*"
Positive exceptions: "*Even though we argue a lot about money, when are we able to talk about money without arguing?*"
Coping statements: "*What do we already know about how to handle these issues successfully?*"

Scaling questions: "*I know we still bicker and criticize each other, but it's happening less frequently (or doesn't last as long, or never gets as bad as it used to).*"

Typical questions that help generate the context of competence are the following:

- *How will we know when you've really been successful with* The STOP Program?
- *After you finish coming here, what kinds of changes do you think you'll continue to make in your life?*
- *What's the first sign you'll be able to notice that* The STOP Program *has been helpful to you?*
- *What's the first sign others will be able to see that* The STOP Program *has been helpful to you?*
- *If you've experienced similar problems before, how did you deal with them?*
- *Tell us about one of the times when you started to lose it, but you stopped it before it went too far?*
- *Can you remember a time recently when you pleasantly surprised yourself or did something out of character that pleased you?*
- *Even though you yelled at your wife, it sounds like you were able to stop yourself from threatening her or becoming physical. How were you successful at stopping yourself here?*
- *Even though you had a big blowout, it sounds like the two of you were able to end it pretty quickly, and after about an hour it was pretty much over. How were the two of you successful at recovering so quickly?*

PACING AND LEADING

One strategy to bypass the inherent defensiveness of the domestic violence offenders in our programs is called "pacing and leading." This approach, originating from the work of Milton Erickson and further developed by neo-Ericksonian practitioners (Erickson & Rossi, 1979; Gilligan, 1987), carefully mirrors the experience of the other person, followed by a "leading" suggestion for a new way to think or act. Based on Erickson's original work with indirect, naturalistic hypnotherapy, pacing means first developing empathy and rapport for the other person's experience by careful delineation prior to making any correction or suggestion, prior to fostering a new perspective, or prior to guiding a new behavior.

Step 1: Offer mirroring responses that confirm the person's experience.

Step 2: Then and only then "lead" him into some new ways of thinking, feeling, or behaving.

In domestic violence groups, "pacing" means carefully reflecting back an understanding of the men's experience:

> *When Karen was talking to this other guy at the party, you must have felt really threatened, like something very important was being taken away from you. And you must have felt betrayed, like "How can she do this to me?" Plus, it was in front of other people, and your pride was at stake. And you felt powerless, probably thinking that "I have to do something about this right now." You probably felt it all through your body, and it felt awful, and you didn't know what to do. It makes sense that you would feel this way, and that you would feel this urge to try to do something to feel powerful again.*

Then, and only then, comes the "lead":

> *And at that point, probably the most powerful thing to do would be to remember that you get insecure in these situations, and that it doesn't always mean that Karen is doing something to you. And to remember that you have ways to talk to her about it afterwards. You can let her know what you need from her.*

There are three kinds of mistakes you can make in "pacing and leading":

Improper pacing: If you tell someone that they are probably very anxious right now, and they are not, then the pacing is off base.

Insufficient pacing: If you make a few pacing statements and the person is still very guarded and mistrusting, it may mean that you need to spend more time with the pacing process.

Improper lead: Even though you may have paced very accurately and successfully, your "lead" suggestion may be something that doesn't make sense or feels offensive in some way to the person.

When in doubt, return to pacing. It is hard to go wrong by doing this.

In the situation above, the inexperienced group leader could have simply stepped in with the obvious "lead"—but without proper pacing, the likely response for the group member would have been something like: "*You don't know what it's like to have her treat me like this!*" Without pacing, the group leader lacks emotional credibility. With pacing, the person is more likely to feel understood, and more receptive to the value of the advice, guidance, or correction.

PROVISIONAL STATUS POLICY (Group Leader's Version)

The following are grounds for placing a group member on *provisional status* in group treatment (leading to possible termination). These criteria are in addition to activity that takes place outside of the group sessions, such as acts of recidivism, substance abuse problems, other criminal behavior, or failure to attend group:

1. **Consistent** put-downs of women or making light of violence (including derogatory language toward women)

2. **Persistent** disruptive or oppositional behavior in group

3. **Consistent** blaming of partner for relationship problems without self-examination

4. **Consistent** lack of participation in group, including failure to complete homework assignments

5. **Consistent** pattern of "telling stories" that sound like bragging about controlling, abusive, or violent behavior, with little or no sign of remorse

6. **Consistent** pattern of inappropriate messages on clothing (such as t-shirts with sexist messages)

If the group member is deemed to be appropriate for provisional status based on the criteria above or other behaviors deemed to be possible grounds for failure, the following steps should be taken:

1. Discuss these concerns directly with the group member. Indicate exactly what you need to see in the future for him to continue in the program. Indicate when his behavior will be reviewed again (usually 1–3 weeks). Depending on clinical judgment, this discussion can take place privately or in the group itself.

2. Follow up with the group member and give feedback indicating either his success in meeting program standards or informing him that you are recommending termination from the program.

It is our policy to attempt to engage group members in the treatment process and to help them correct unacceptable behaviors if possible. Strategies for intervening when group members are engaging in these behaviors include the following:

- At first, give the benefit of the doubt and assume ignorance: "*You may not be aware of this, but . . .*" or "*I don't think you realize how this comes across, but . . .*"

- Try to keep the interventions as benign and respectful as possible. Remember that these men are feeling shamed and defensive, and they are often testing us to see what they can get away with.

- As much as possible, state the rules as clearly and simply as possible.

- Employ pacing and leading whenever possible. Make sure that the group member feels that his point is recognized and respected, even if you are correcting his behavior. Continue to remind the group members that, although their complaints about their partners, job, or legal system may be valid, the purpose of this group is for them to examine themselves.

- If a problem behavior is developing, catch it as early as possible in the group member's treatment. Patterns of problem behavior should be noted and confronted no later than sessions 6 to 8 for an individual group member. For example, make a comment the first time someone talks about the way "all women" are.

- However, be careful about confronting problem behavior too early. Many of these men need to have room to be defensive and oppositional early on and often come around on their own.

- If the group leader is feeling intimidated by a nucleus of group members who are disruptive, discuss this with colleagues. In these situations, it is often wise to meet privately with problem group members to enlist their alliance with the group goals and also to issue a general (not aimed at a single person) statement to the group about what is expected from the group.

- If one member is being difficult, the leader may choose to discuss this in the group, so that other group members can see that someone is taking charge of the direction of the group. Other group members also may have valuable feedback for this group member. However, the strategies for handling these situations are clinical, case-by-case decisions.

- Remember that the group leader is fully empowered to recommend that a group member be terminated from group. This does not represent a failure of the program or the group leaders.

THE BROKEN MIRROR
A Self Psychological Treatment Perspective for Relationship Violence

The first four to six months we were together, I thought I was just walking on water. Everything I did was wonderful. Everything about me was cool. I felt great. It was almost like I looked at her and I would always feel great about myself. And then it all came crashing down. She doesn't look at me the same way anymore. The kids demand a lot of attention. It's like she doesn't think I'm that great anymore. So now, I don't even talk to her about a lot of things because they might upset her and mess up her picture of me even more—even when I know that she'll get even madder at me later for lying to her. And then I get mad at her, like it's her fault that I don't feel like I walk on water any more!

One time my son, when he was nine, was trying to do this bike stunt where he would have to make his bike jump in the air and then come down over some boards. He couldn't do it. He was scared. I really got on him: "You're a baby, you're chicken, you're weak. I'm going to take your bike away from you!" I kept thinking he was letting me down! It was like he was disrespecting me.

When a man comes home to his wife and children, he expects that something will take place in the transaction between them that will offer him a state of emotional well-being, or what is referred to in self psychology as a state of self-cohesion. The need for self-cohesion is primary. Its origins lie in the original needs between the infant or young child and the most central attachment figure, usually the mother. The child has a compelling need to look into the face of his mother and see, reflected back to him, eyes that say "You are wonderful" and a smile that says "You make me happy."

This is his magic mirror, and the figure in the mirror is known in self psychology theory as the mirroring selfobject. The self psychology theory of normal child development (Shapiro, 1995) states that all children, at some point in their development, need validation and acknowledgment from parental figures. Over time, these lead to the child's capacity to feel pride and take pleasure in his or her accomplishments—to feel a sense of competence and efficacy.

Children who are deprived of these essential responses, or who instead are subjected to criticism and ridicule for the efforts to achieve, become arrested in their development of an internal sense of confidence and competence. As adults, they are

Excerpted with permission from *Journal of Psychotherapy Practice and Research*, 8(2), 1999; Wexler (1999).

always looking to some outside source of approval or recognition (mirroring). But no mother, no father, no teacher, no coach, and no therapist ever provide the perfect mirror. Some of these mirroring figures, as we all know rather too well, are often quite fragmented themselves and have little capacity to offer the loving and self-enhancing reflection that the child desperately requires. Or, in some cases, a mismatch between child and mirror figure takes place such that the child eternally feels a lack of understanding, a dearth of genuine appreciation, and a fundamental gap in attunement. Even in the best of situations, this relationship can be experienced as incomplete. The child thus develops gaps in his sense of self: he mistrusts and disrespects his own internal signals and states; he doubts his own self-worth and competence. He desperately turns elsewhere for validation and, even more than most of us, he becomes excessively sensitized to signals that might suggest that he is unappreciated, unneeded, or unsuccessful.

Thus, the adult man who has been deprived of these essential mirroring functions turns, unconsciously, to his closest adult relationships and activities to help him acquire what was never soundly established long ago. He enters a love relationship with defenses erected against too much intimacy, for fear of being hurt and missing attunement once again. The needs resurface, inevitably, as the emotional connection develops. He hopes, he prays, that the good feelings he has about himself as he intertwines his life with his partner and family will buoy him for the rest of his life against the emptiness and deprivation that he has already experienced.

Some of this psychology can best be understood from an understanding of the power to generate a state of self-cohesion and well-being that men in our culture frequently offer women. Pleck (1980) outlines two very important dimensions of male reliance on female validation.

The first is that men perceive women as having *expressive power,* the power to express emotions. Many men have learned to depend on women to help them express emotions; in fact, women's richer emotional life and capacity for emotional expression provides an essential life spark for many men. Whether they can identify this or not, many men feel lost without the fundamental connection to this spark.

The second form of reliance is *masculinity-validating* power. Men depend on women to remind them, and reassure them, of their fundamental masculinity and masculine self-worth. When a woman refuses to offer this validation, or when a man's unrealistic expectations and subsequent distortions convince him that she is withholding this, many men feel lost. They desperately demand the restoration of their virility, masculinity, self-worth, and, ultimately, self-cohesion, by the powerful confirming source. Thus, the reflection offered by these female mirrors is extremely powerful. And the man who craves mirroring finds, as the relationship moves on, that his wife, and now his children, and the job he has, and the life they have together have not sufficiently made up for what he has never received. When his wife seems more interested in talking to her sister than to him, and when their sex life wanes, and when his children do not show the respect to their parents that he envisioned, he becomes fragmented. When these responses are not forthcoming, these men are unable to maintain their sense of self-worth, self-esteem, or validity. Various types of behaviors reflecting this fragmentation may ensue (gambling, substance abuse, reckless sexual behavior, aggression, etc.).

White and Weiner (1986) offer a valuable description from the self psychological perspective of the experience of the abusive parent, which is quite parallel to the experience of the frustrated, abusive husband. They identify the narcissistic rage over the inability to *make* the child react as if he or she were part of the parent's self and really know what was wanted. Here, the mirroring selfobject function is extremely important, and quite fragile. So long as a child (or partner) provides the appreciation needed, self-esteem is maintained. When the applause fails, the narcissistic rage erupts along with an inner experience of a fragmenting self. The narcissistically impaired adult needs to be respected and obeyed and made to feel worthwhile; when he does not see that positive reflection in the interpersonal mirror, he is left feeling vulnerable, helpless, and outraged.

> *I've been married 10 years. The first six years were picture perfect. We had little spats, but that was all. But then this thing called parenthood came along. She was more critical of me, plus the heat from my career got way turned up. And she just got more and more of an attitude. And I'm thinking, "You're not the only one entitled to have an attitude." I became the sole breadwinner, and instead of making her an equal partner in our lives, my "father" came out of me.*
>
> *I just became my dad! Instead of looking at the fact that she was stressed out, I just blew up. Everything that I had said I would never do, I did anyway!*
>
> *I can drink myself into oblivion just to escape from my feelings. Of course, I can be just as mean sober. I have developed this incredibly painful jaw and neck. It can ruin my night. It has everything to do with all this stress and anger and attitude.*

Some disappointment like this is inevitable in the course of human relationships and the recognition of limits. **The problem with the man who becomes abusive with his partner or children is that he has mistaken the flood of good feelings that comes from a close relationship with a promise that the good mirror will always shine.** So, in his eyes, the mirror breaks, his sense of self shatters, and he blames the mirror. **Because she promised.**

Stosny (1995) describes these men as "attachment abusers." When they see reflected back to them an image that makes them feel unlovable or inadequate, they feel ashamed. They blame the mirror for the reflection.

Some of these men become psychologically, sexually, emotionally, or physically abusive with their partners—because these psychological vulnerabilities, in combination with other social and environmental factors, set the stage for abusive acts in relationships. Dutton's (Dutton & Golant, 1995) research on the origins of male battering identifies the ways in which socialization combines with psychological influences to create an abusive personality: Contributing factors include a sense of powerlessness in early childhood, the experience of having been shamed and battered, and couples with insecure avoidant–ambivalent bonding styles. Men who scored the highest for "fearful attachment" also scored highest for jealousy. "Jealousy," the authors note, "is the terror of abandonment" (p. 139). They go on to demonstrate that these fears are at the center of many abusive acts.

The treatment implications of this are profound. The clinician who can genuinely understand the perpetrator's unmet needs for mirroring and affirmation—and who can suspend preoccupation with moralistically rejecting the immature and unacceptable forms through which these were expressed—is potentially of tremendous value. The selfobject needs of the perpetrator are *valid.* Recognizing how the behaviors that he chooses are intended to regain self-cohesion and some sense of power and control *over his crumbling sense of self* (not necessarily over *another person*) leads to a new, more accessible, and deeply respectful therapeutic encounter.

If we understand the driving force behind many of these men, we can recognize that most of them (with some notable exceptions, as will be explained below) are not that different from most other men or women. Their actions may violate moral or legal codes and may not be in the behavioral repertoire of many other adults, but the fundamental emotions, needs, and struggles are certainly not unique or foreign. The task of clinicians and educators, in offering treatment, is to understand this pattern and to offer these men a new narrative of themselves and a new set of tools for coping with these very human experiences. The self psychology perspective (Shapiro, 1995; White & Weiner, 1986), which emphasizes the breakdowns in the *experience* of self-cohesion leading to desperate acts, offers us a map.

SHAME

Dutton's model (Dutton & Golant, 1995) for understanding the multiple factors which set the stage for domestic violence is particularly illuminating about the male psychological experience. And it especially allows us to develop a more empathic understanding of these men. Dutton outlined several key background factors that set the stage for a boy growing up to become a man who batters. Although this paradigm was developed based on studies of only one category (emotionally volatile/Type III), the principles significantly overlap into the other categories as well. Dutton explains how the seeds come from three distinct sources: being shamed (especially by one's father), an insecure attachment to one's mother, and the direct observation of abusiveness in the home.

According to Dutton, shaming comes from public exposure of one's vulnerability. The whole self feels "bad." Abused children often shut off all emotion, to defend against rage and hurt at perpetrator. A father who shames has a need to punish. When he attacks his son, he is desperately attempting to regain some lost sense of self, to bolster or reassure his own shaky sense of self. For the boy who needs to feel loved by this main source of his male identity, it is a series of crushing blows.

> *My father used to put me down. He slapped me around, called me "shit for brains," told me he should have never had me. Now I get it. When my wife says something that sounds even a little bit critical, I hear the same damn thing in my head: "shit for brains, shit for brains . . ."*
>
> *If I stacked something wrong in the store, he'd slap me upside the head in front of other people. He would call me stupid. I was always nervous about the type of job I was doing. He would slap me if I screwed up until I got it right.*
>
> *I was a good enough athlete to play college ball in three sports—but he would always criticize me. I once got a whipping for not winning a race—he thought I hadn't put out full effort. The way my father brought me up caused me more problems. I'm not satisfied with who I am and I never will be.*

People who have been exposed to shame will do anything to avoid it in the future. They develop a hypersensitive radar to the possibility of humiliation, and they are almost phobic in their overreactivity. They tend to project blame and perceive the worst in others. These men are, tragically, usually the ones most desperate for affection and approval but they cannot ask for it. Sometimes the smallest signs of withdrawal of affection will activate the old narcissistic wounds—and they lash out at the perceived source of this new wound. They can describe none of these feelings; they don't even know where they have come from.

Furthermore, if the mother of this young child is only intermittently capable of offering emotional connection and support, he spends too much time trying to bring her closer; this drains him of the attention, energy, and confidence needed for moving forward developmentally. Conversely, if she is too anxious and needs too much attention or validation from *him,* she intrudes upon him and he cannot separate. He never fully develops an inner sense of a lovable, stable, valuable core self. This boy develops an ambivalent attitude toward her and later toward women in general: they are the providers of essential emotional life-support, but they are only intermittently trustworthy and available.

As attachment is necessary for survival, the male learns early that his mother (and, by association, any intimate woman) has monumental power over him. True emotional safety and security are initially associated with the physical presence of a woman—but it is only inconsistently available. As adults, these men try to diminish their anxiety about being abandoned by exaggerated control of their female partner.

> *With my wife—she gets on me about moving the furniture, that I'm not doing it right: "You always do this, you never do that, you never think about anyone else, you're only thinking about yourself. . . ." The leg of the sofa breaks, now I'm the dummy who did it. She runs me down about money. But I excel at lots of things, and I seem to get criticized anyway. The minute she gives me any sort of criticism, I get mad enough to fight.*

As Dutton (Dutton & Golant, 1995) describes it, "A boy with an absent or punitive father and a demanding but unavailable mother learns that men don't give emotional comfort, and that women appear to be supportive but are ultimately demanding and can't be trusted" (p. 114).

This is the cry of the little boy within the grown man: "Why can't she make me feel better?"

When these psychological variables are combined with the observation of abusive behavior in the home, we have a future prescription for male relationship violence. Research studies have indicated that males who witnessed parents attacking each other were three to four times more likely to eventually assault their wives (Straus, Gelles, & Steinmetz, 1980). Although being on the receiving end of physical and emotional abuse is a prominent variable in the population of spouse abusers, witnessing male–female adult abuse is even more significant (Hotaling & Sugarman, 1986; Kalmuss, 1984).

SELF PSYCHOLOGY APPROACHES: THE SELF-OBJECT PERSPECTIVE

Several concepts from self psychology are especially valuable in making sense of the spouse abuser's experience and in guiding treatment interventions. First and foremost is the concept of the mirroring selfobject (Shapiro, 1995; White & Weiner, 1986; Wolf, 1988; Wolfe, 1989). When a child looks into the eyes of his parent and sees reflected back to him a loving and approving look, his basic sense of himself is deeply validated. He feels alive and worthy. When an adult male in a relationship looks into the eyes of his partner and sees reflected back to him a look of love and delight and profound respect, he likewise feels alive and worthy. However, since this perfect mirroring inevitably—even in the best of relationships—wears off, at least to some degree, this man is doomed to a cracking of the mirror and a cracking of the self. It is this experience that must be identified and owned for many men who turn on their partners. They need to understand the origin of their deep unrest and their deep resentment so they can position themselves to possibly take some responsibility for it. As with most other psychological experiences, the identified and known experience has a profound organizing effect and allows the individual to respond more maturely and appropriately to the genuine problem. The twinship selfobject is a much more adaptive experience at this point in the relationship. This would allow a husband to say to his wife, *"'Y' know, I feel really lost sometimes without all the special times we had together. It just seems like having kids and getting used to each other and money problems have really taken their toll. I guess you must feel the same way."* Here the man has shifted his primary need from the mirroring function of his partner to one in which they are profoundly alike. She is no longer the enemy, but rather a comrade along the difficult road of life—a comrade who is inevitably flawed, but no more fundamentally flawed than he.

Also from the self psychology perspective, it is important to recognize the fundamental narcissistic injury or selfobject breakdown that usually precedes an outbreak of abusive behavior. In fact, we can usually observe the effects of an injury to the vulnerable self in the clinical relationship, since there is inevitably an empathic failure in all treatment experiences. The research of Holtzworth-Munroe and Hutchinson (1993) is particularly illuminating here. They examined the "misattributions" of men who abuse their wives compared to a nonabusive male population. They found that violent husbands were much more likely to attribute the most negative intentions to their wives' behavior: when presented vignettes of situations like a wife talking to another man at a party or a wife who is not interested in sex on a particular night, these men were much more likely to be convinced that she was *trying* to make the man angry, hurt his feelings, put him down, get something for herself, or pick a fight. The researchers also found that when the men *perceived* a situation of abandon-ment or rejection, they were particularly likely to generate incompetent behavioral responses. These are narcissistic injuries to these men; and, as with all narcissistic injuries, they are strictly governed by the cognitive interpretation of the event. A nonviolent husband might interpret the same situation in a different, more benign way. If his wife were spending a lot of time talking to another man at a party, he might be irritated at her, or he might make nothing of it, or he might actually feel pleased that she was attractive and popular and having a good time. This recognition of the vulnerability to narcissistic injury—and the ability to communicate this understanding in the clinical setting—allow both us and these men in treatment to develop a greater respect for how their hurt feelings and eventual desperate reactions developed.

The clinical goal here is to create an "experience-near" intervention; with this population, that must elicit the man's experience of being *powerless*, no matter how much the political analysis as observed from outside indicates that he is *powerful*. Harway and Evans (1996) critique one of the foundation pieces of the domestic violence models: Walker's "Cycle of Violence" (Walker, 1984). The original cycle identifies the stages that some spousal battering patterns go through: escalation to explosion to honeymoon period. Both man and woman tend to deny the problems of the other stages because of the sweetness and satisfaction of the honeymoon period—but, tragically, the escalation period inevitably reemerges, culminating in explosion once more. According to Walker, this cycle tends to become shorter and shorter, with more frequent and more disturbing periods of escalation and explosion.

More recent research suggests that many couples do *not* experience this pattern of more rapid cycling and more dangerous intensity (Johnson, 1995). Many couples have occasional incidents of abuse that do not inevitably lead to more danger. And, certainly, many men do not *experience* this cycle in the way that is described. The fact that they do not experience it this way does not invalidate it, but it certainly does not lend itself to being a valuable intervention. To confront men in treatment with the cycle of violence model as *the* quintessential pattern of abuse—with its emphasis on male domination and inevitable escalation—causes us to lose much of our audience. Many of these men do not feel that this accurately describes them and they become defensive or, even worse, disengaged.

Instead, Harway and Evans (1996) use the "Cycle of Feeling Avoidance." This model reflects the more typical—and often surprising—experience of powerlessness that men have in difficult interpersonal relationships. Many men—and certainly many men who become abusive—have very low tolerance for difficult or aversive feelings (Gottman, 1994). When they experience some personal injury or discomfort, they feel overwhelmed. A mistake may lead to shame, frustration to helplessness, emotional distance to loneliness. In this model, men do *whatever it takes* to defend against these extremely dysphoric states. They may behave with passivity, such as placating or excessive apologizing just to keep the peace. Or they may take a more active approach, as men in our culture are oriented to do: lashing out at the person who seems to be causing this pain, engaging in controlling behavior to eliminate the sources of discomfort, abusing substances as an escape from the feelings, acting out recklessly (such as sexual escapades or dangerous driving) to provide some relief.

> *So here I am, in this kind of frenzy, I guess, pretending to wave this razor blade around. It wasn't even in my hand, but she thought it was. And I can hear this screaming my head: "You don't care about me!" "I want to have control over SOMETHING in my life!" And later I thought about how I had been adopted, and how I didn't even get to "choose" my real parents; they made that decision for me.*

In this state, under these circumstances, the other people in this man's life are perceived *only* as potential selfobject figures. His wife's behavior, feelings, and "independent center of initiative" are peripheral to the fundamental drive for self-cohesion: he will do *anything it takes* to avoid the dysphoria and regain some measure of well-being. Often this means gaining control over someone else. And often this means emotional, verbal, or physical abuse.

In the treatment setting, clinicians can offer these men a new, stable, mirroring selfobject—so that they can feel a deeper sense of self-respect and can maintain a more grounded sense of self as they deal with the emotional minefield inherent in many love relationships. And they can offer them a new, mature twinship experience—so that they can recognize that we are similar passengers on this journey through sensitive episodes and difficult moments in relationships. While many of us would not turn to physically abusive or emotionally intimidating behavior, we at least share the experience of feeling hurt and threatened and occasionally resorting to behaviors in response to these states that we deeply regret. In this way, clinicians and clients can experience twinship.

PART II
SPECIAL PROGRAM SESSIONS

ORIENTATION SESSION GUIDELINES

The *STOP Program* orientation session is designed to be administered to all new group members entering at the once monthly new group member session. This information should be presented by both group therapists and should be scheduled for 45 minutes prior to the group session. The orientation session may be used with a single new group member or a small group of new members.

Theories about group counseling (Yalom, 1995) suggest that pregroup preparation is essential for a successful group experience. The purpose of this orientation is to familiarize the new members with the basic policies of the program. It is also designed to acquaint them with the particular expectations about group interactions and to address typical concerns that new members have in entering new groups.

1. Review of group rules and regulations (see "Orientation Information/FAQs")

2. Explore concerns of group members
   a. Discuss previous experiences in groups
   b. Review FAQs

3. Clarify evaluation/expectations of group members
   a. Review "Provisional Status Policy"

4. Clarify group themes
   a. Review the "Nine Commandments"
   b. Introduce "Feelings Count"

ORIENTATION INFORMATION/FAQs

Welcome to *The STOP Program*. The following is a list of answers to frequently asked questions about the groups. Please read this information carefully.

1. *Why was I referred to The STOP Program?* You were referred to this program because of reports that you were involved in one or more incidents of relationship violence. The fact that you have been referred to *The STOP Program* indicates that this problem is treatable.

2. *How often do the groups meet?* Each group meets for two hours, once a week for 52 weeks.

3. *Who else is in the group?* The group members include men like yourself who have been involved in some sort of relationship violence. This is an ongoing group; one session each month is designated as a new member session in which new members are introduced to the group. It is very valuable to have group members at different stages of treatment to help explain to a new member how the group works.

4. *What happens in the group?* Our philosophy is that men who get into trouble in their relationships need to learn new skills. We want to make sure that you have new ways of handling stress, new ways of thinking about difficult relationship situations, and new ways of problem solving. When you leave this program, you should have lots of new tools that will help you handle things differently. This will make it much less likely that the same problems will take place again.

   Each session is designed to focus on a particular aspect of relationship health or relationship violence. Groups provide an atmosphere for members to discuss the problems they have encountered, the feelings that have led to the destructive behavior, and the impact violence has had on the relationship. New ways of understanding yourself, understanding others, and relating to other people are strongly emphasized.

5. *Is this a class or group counseling?* Although many of the group sessions may involve teaching of specific skills, such as stress management and improved communication, the groups are considered to be group counseling. This means that there is a strong emphasis placed on self-examination, discussion of feelings, and support for other group members. Most people benefit from the group based on how committed they are to engage in these tasks.

6. *Do I have to come every week?* You are required to attend every week. Research indicates that there is a direct relationship between steady attendance and treatment progress. In order for you to benefit from the program, attendance must a priority for you. As you become more involved in the group, you will probably find out that you are motivated to attend, not only for your own benefit, but also to support your fellow group members.

7. *What about absences?* We recognize that there may be circumstances that require you to miss a group session. If you are unable to attend a group session, please notify our staff beforehand to let us know that you will be unable to attend. Documentation of all absences is required and should be given to our staff prior to your absence. If you miss a group session for unexpected reasons, please bring in documentation for the absence at the next group session. Undocumented absences will be considered unexcused.

   Unexcused absences indicate a lack of interest or commitment to change your situation. An unexcused absence will be grounds for a report back to your probation officer or other referring agency, which may result in the termination of treatment.

8. *What happens if I arrive late?* If a group member arrives more than 5 minutes late, he will be marked as late. Three times late will be treated as the equivalent of one unexcused absence. If a group member arrives 15 or more minutes late, he will (under no circumstances) be allowed into the group, and this will be considered an unexcused absence.

9. *Who leads the groups?* All of the group leaders are certified domestic violence counselors who have had extensive training in treatment of relationship violence.

10. *Are there additional expectations for successful participation other than group attendance?* All sessions have homework assignments which you will be expected to complete and bring to the next group meeting. The group leaders will assign homework at the end of each group meeting so you will know what is expected. The group leaders will also discuss the previous session's completed homework at the beginning of each group meeting. Three missed homework assignments will be considered the equivalent of one unexcused absence. This will be grounds for a report back to your probation officer or other referring agency, which may result in the termination of treatment.

    Group members are required to be at the site 10 minutes before the time for the group to start in order to fill out a questionnaire, "Weekly Check-in." Group will not begin until everyone completes the questionnaire.

    You will be given a binder, titled *Handouts and Homework*, at the first group meeting. Each week, information from the *Handouts and Homework* binder will be discussed during the group session. You are expected to bring your binder to each group meeting.

11. *What about confidentiality? Can what I say in the group be used against me?* Because this treatment uses a team approach, you can assume that what you say in the group may be discussed with your probation officer or other referring agency. Only information directly related to your treatment goals is included in these reports. Most of the personal issues and feelings discussed in the group sessions remain confidential.

    In certain situations, the group leaders are obligated to report information that is revealed in the group. These reportable situations include serious threats of hurting or killing someone else, serious threats of hurting or killing yourself, new and significant reports of family violence (including incidents in which children have witnessed spousal abuse), child abuse, or elder abuse.

12. *What about new incidents of violence in my relationship?* As a participant in domestic violence treatment you are expected to discuss any new incidents of violence in your relationships. Presenting information about new incidents of violence does not necessarily lead to termination if you genuinely appear to be remorseful, take responsibility for your actions, and appear to be making efforts to prevent similar reoccurrences in the future. Keep in mind that it is in your best interest to disclose a new incident of violence. When these incidents are discovered through other sources, it impacts negatively on you.

13. *What about electronic devices?* During the group session, please turn off all electronic devices. You will have an opportunity during the 10-minute midsession break to return pages or phone messages.

14. *How should I dress for the group?* There is no specific dress code for these sessions. However, no clothing with inappropriate messages promoting or making light of sexist or violent behavior, or otherwise inappropriate content, will be permitted in the group sessions.

15. *Any other rules about appropriate behavior?* While on the premises of this agency, you are asked to use respectful language which is not offensive to staff or other clients being served. There is to be no use of alcohol prior to the group session. Group members will not threaten or intimidate any group members or leaders at any time.

16. *Won't group counseling try and get me to let out all my emotions? I'm not comfortable with that!* Everybody in group counseling is different, and each person decides how much of his personal

emotions to reveal to others. No one is expected to walk right in and talk about their deepest feelings in front of a bunch of strangers.

Over time, most people become more and more comfortable letting the group know more about what is happening inside them. We know that there is usually a correlation between talking about yourself and getting some benefit from the sessions. But this all happens at the pace of the individual.

17. *Can I have individual counseling instead? I don't like talking in front of other people and I can get more personal attention.* The STOP Program philosophy is that these kinds of problems are best treated in a group setting. You get the benefit of hearing about the experiences of others and learning from their successes and mistakes. The feedback from peers is one of the single most important factors in predicting positive outcome.

18. *Why do I need to be in a group with a bunch of spouse abusers? I'm not like them!* We treat the man, not the label. We stay away from labels that sound like put-downs. Instead, we focus on the specific thoughts, feelings, and situations that have led to problem behaviors. We could put any man in this group, regardless of what has gone wrong in his behavior with others, and he would benefit from the approaches used in this treatment model.

I have read the above information and agree to the conditions of treatment.

_____   _____
Group Member's Signature   Print Name

_____   _____
Date   Group Name

PROVISIONAL STATUS POLICY (GROUP MEMBER'S VERSION)

 Handout

The following are grounds for group members to be placed on provisional status in *The STOP Program* (leading to possible termination). These behaviors are in addition to activity that takes place outside of the group sessions, such as acts of violence, repeated drug or alcohol problems, or failure to attend group:

1. **Consistently** putting down women or minimizing violence

2. **Persistent** disruptive or oppositional behavior in group

3. **Consistent** blaming of partner for relationship problems without self-examination

4. **Consistent** lack of participation in group, including failure to complete homework assignments

5. **Consistent** pattern of "telling stories" (bragging or showing off) about controlling, abusive, or violent behavior with little or no sign of remorse

6. **Consistent** pattern of inappropriate messages on clothing (such as t-shirts with sexist messages)

THE NINE COMMANDMENTS

 **Handout**

1. We are all 100% responsible for our own behavior.

2. Violence is not an acceptable solution to problems.

3. We do not have control over any other person, but we do have control over ourselves.

4. When communicating with someone else, we need to express our feelings directly rather than blaming or threatening.

5. Increased awareness of self-talk, physical cues, and emotions is essential for progress and improvement.

6. We can always take a time-out before reacting.

7. We can't do anything about the past, but we can change the future.

8. Although there are differences between men and women, our needs and rights are fundamentally alike.

9. Counselors and case managers cannot make people change—they can only set the stage for change to occur.

FEELINGS COUNT

 Handout

HAPPY AND CONFIDENT

Accepted	Alive	Brave	Calm	Caring	Cheerful
Comfortable	Confident	Excited	Friendly	Fulfilled	Generous
Grateful	Happy	Hopeful	Joyful	Lovable	Loving
Peaceful	Playful	Powerful	Proud	Relaxed	Relieved
Respected	Secure	Understood	Valuable	Warm	Worthwhile

FEAR AND WORRY

Anxious	Apprehensive	Confused	Desperate	Distrustful
Fearful	Helpless	Horrified	Inhibited	Out-of-Control
Overwhelmed	Panicky	Pressured	Threatened	Trapped
Troubled	Uncertain	Uneasy/Uptight	Vulnerable	Worried

ANGRY AND RESENTFUL

Angry	Bitter	Contemptuous	Disgusted	Disrespected	
Frustrated	Furious	Hostile/Impatient	Irritated	Outraged	
Provoked	Resentful	Stubborn	Unappreciated	Used	Victimized

SAD AND PESSIMISTIC

Confused	Defeated	Depressed	Devastated	Disappointed	Miserable
Discouraged	Helpless	Hopeless	Isolated	Lonely	
Overwhelmed	Sad	Stuck	Trapped	Useless	

UNCOMFORTABLE AND INSECURE

Awkward	Embarrassed	Foolish	Humiliated	Inhibited
Insecure	Self-conscious	Shy	Uncomfortable	

APOLOGETIC AND GUILTY

Apologetic	Guilty	Remorseful	Sorry	Untrustworthy

HURT AND REJECTED

Devastated	Excluded	Hurt	Ignored	Rejected	Vulnerable

JEALOUS AND LEFT OUT

Envious	Deprived	Left out	Jealous

ASHAMED AND INADEQUATE

Ashamed	Inferior	Inadequate	Incompetent	Stupid
Useless	Unattractive	Unworthy	Powerless	

New Member Session 1
HOUSE OF ABUSE

This material (or the material from New Member Session 2) should be presented only when one or more group members are beginning the program, then the regularly scheduled group content should resume.

New Member Session 1 and New Member Session 2 should each be presented in alternate months.

MATERIALS

"House of Abuse"

GOAL

To introduce group members to the basic definitions of abuse and the range of intimidating behaviors.

TASKS

1. *Conduct dyad exercise.*
2. *Explain "House of Abuse."*
3. *Identify different "rooms" of the House.*

PROGRAM

1. In this session, all group members should split up into dyads; interviewing each other *only* about basic information. This is *not* the time to ask about or report information about the offense that led to their assignment to this program:

   Please pair up with one of the group members next to you. You will have a few minutes each to get some basic information from your "partner": What is his name? Is he currently married or together with his partner? What is her name? Does he have kids? What are their names and ages? Where is he from? What kind of work does he do? What are his interests and hobbies? What does he expect to get out of this group? What does he think he can add to the group? You don't need to find out any details about how your partner here ended up in the group. We save that for much later. Then you and your "partner" will introduce each other to the group.

At the end of this, and throughout the early group sessions, group leaders should seek out ways to establish connections among group members, such as those who are parents, those who are from similar parts of the country, or do similar types of work.

Even if many of the men have already been through this exercise previously, they should still pair up with a new partner and go through it again.

Remember that because of intermittent attendance many of the group members may be new to each other, even if this is not their own first session.

It is usually best to keep personal abuse and violence information to a minimum in the first session for a new group member.

2. Begin explaining the basic concept of the "House of Abuse" by drawing a diagram of the "House of Abuse" on the board. By the end of this program, the following categories will be listed in the different rooms:

   - Physical Abuse
   - Verbal/Emotional/Psychological
   - Social Isolation
   - Gender Privilege
   - Intimidation
   - Religion
   - Sexual Abuse
   - Child Abuse

3. It is also important to repeatedly emphasize the "100% rule." This rule states that we are each 100% responsible for our own behavior. Being angry or hurt does not have to lead to abuse or intimidation.

   It has proven very valuable in this exercise to develop descriptions which are as gender-neutral as possible. Most of these forms of destructive conflicts can just as easily be used by a woman to a man as the other way around, with the obvious exceptions of, for the most part, sexual abuse. The goal here is to open up valuable discussion and to help the group members discuss these issues without feeling defensive.

4. Begin by asking for a definition of the most obvious kinds of destructive conflict, or abusive behavior, from one person in a relationship to another—this will usually involve physical abuse and probably yelling and screaming. Ask the question: *"What are some ways that someone in an intimate adult relationship could be destructive or abusive to his or her partner? How can somebody abuse another?"* As the group identifies different themes, label the different rooms, and fill in some of the examples in the room where they best fit.

   Below are some basic descriptions of what belongs in each room:

1. **Physical Abuse.** This is the easiest to identify. This includes any kind of physical aggressive contact, including hitting, choking, or pushing. Make sure to review every possible form that the group can generate. The group members usually describe this first.

2. **Verbal/emotional/psychological.** This is also easy to identify. This includes any kind of name-calling, verbal put-downs, or criticism. This also involves the use of mind games. When a man "teases" a woman about her weight or body and then protests that he was only kidding or only asking a question, he is committing psychological abuse. When she humiliates him in public, she is doing the same thing. Often, men drill home the message that "you could never make it

without me." When people hear this enough times, they may begin to believe it. Humiliating someone for not being successful or competent at something is psychological abuse. Another form of destructive conflict in this category is to ignore someone: the silent treatment. This can be one of the most powerful mind games of all, wearing someone down until they desperately try to "be good."

3. **Social isolation.** This category is often overlooked. This is more typically used by men against women but could work the other way around. Because they feel threatened, men may become determined to prevent their wife or partner from becoming independent or successful. This may involve sabotaging the woman's attempts to work, go to school, or have friends or activities of her own. The fear for a man here is that the woman won't need him anymore if she develops in this way. This is the ultimate indication of insecurity—the man has to keep her down so that he can feel more confident and dominant.

4. **Gender privilege**. The male gender privilege form of destructive conflicts includes the entitlement men claim that leads them to dominate the relationship. The man who insists on using the fact that he is the breadwinner to demand that he make decisions for the marriage and family would be an example. This same attitude can be used to demand sex, get out of household chores, or demand more control over his free time than his wife or partner is allowed. A man may tell his wife or partner that he "needs" to go away with his buddies for a week; what would it be like if she told him the same thing, and if she just assumed that he would watch the kids and take care of business at home?

    The female gender privilege form of destructive conflicts includes the female's insistence that she have more control over child-rearing decisions or the color of the new sofa. If a woman insists that she shouldn't have to work because *that's the man's job*, we have an example of female gender privilege.

5. **Intimidation.** This includes threats to kill or hurt the other person, threats against the kids, or threats of kidnapping the kids. It may involve telling her that a judge will never give her custody because she's crazy or she doesn't work or she has used drugs in the past. Threatening suicide is another example of intimidation—this can be a very powerful way of controlling someone because they are desperate to avoid the terrible guilt and pain. The goal of these gambits is to produce *fear*, which is used to maintain dominance and control.

6. **Religion.** Using religion as a form of abuse involves invoking the Bible or other religious work as a rationalization for domination. It should be pointed out that, like statistics, religious works can be interpreted as an explanation for just about anything. Be careful here—making remarks which might seem disrespectful about any religion can be very damaging to initial rapport. It is often helpful to start out by suggesting that one form of destructive conflict can consist of restricting a partner's right to attend his or her house of worship, or insisting that she participate in religious observances when she doesn't want to. As the discussion moves on, try asking the question, "How could someone use the Bible as a form of abuse"

7. **Sexual Abuse**. The most blatant form of sexual abuse is rape, which has only recently been declared a crime in a marriage in all states. However, this is not the only form of sexual abuse in a relationship. Demanding that the partner watch or read pornography can be abusive. Insisting on certain sex acts that she finds humiliating or degrading can be abusive.

8. **Child Abuse.** Any physical, sexual, verbal, or emotional form of child abuse is likewise an abuse to the marriage. Using the kids as pawns in the battle between parents or threatening to hurt the kids would be examples here also. This can often lead to a discussion about the ways in which abused children often become abusers themselves in the next generation.

   After establishing the rooms in the "House of Abuse," ask the group members to consider the following questions:

   "Is this a house that you would like to live in?"

   "You don't have to say anything out loud, but see if you recognize any of these rooms as rooms in your house right now."

   "Again, don't say anything out loud, but see if you recognize any of these rooms as rooms in the house you grew up in."

   "Would you say that most of the examples we have come up with constitute illegal or criminal behavior? If not, then be aware that we are defining abusive behavior in relationships as anything which is clearly hurtful or destructive in this relationship—even if you can't go to jail for it."

THE HOUSE OF ABUSE*

Handout

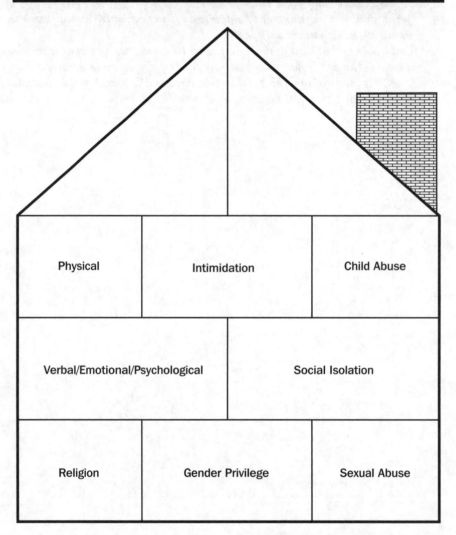

The House of Abuse*

Physical	Intimidation	Child Abuse
Verbal/Emotional/Psychological		Social Isolation
Religion	Gender Privilege	Sexual Abuse

*The House of Abuse chart was developed by Michael F. McGrane, MSW, LICSW, Director of the Violence Prevention & Intervention Services (VPIS) of the Amherst H. Wilder Foundation, and is used here by permission. The chart is part of a complete domestic abuse curriculum entitled *Foundations for Violence-Free Living: A Step-by-Step Guide to Facilitating Men's Domestic Abuse Groups*, available from Fieldstone Alliance at 1-800-274-6024.

New Member Session 2
TIME-OUT

MATERIALS

"Time-out"
"Time-out Information for Partners"
"When Your Partner Blocks Your Path"

GOAL

To introduce group members to the time-out strategies to avert relationship abusive.

TASKS

1. *Conduct dyad exercise.*
2. *Review "Time-out."*
3. *Review "Time-out Information for Partners."*
4. *Review "When Your Partner Blocks Your Path."*

PROGRAM

See instructions for dyad exercise on page 38, and conduct the same way here.

Time-out

1. Introduce the idea of having a plan for episodes when it feels as though behavior is getting out of control. This requires personal responsibility—to recognize the signals and to act responsibly in those situations. The odds of being successful with this plan are much higher when people have thought about it, planned for it, and rehearsed it in advance.

2. Review "Time-out": This technique does not help the couple resolve the issue at hand; thus, it is a stopgap measure. However, it often prevents violence, which is the primary goal. Communication skills can be learned later, after the fear of any destructive behavior (verbal or physical abuse) is gone.

43

Model the use of the skill with a co-leader or one of the group members. Make sure that the group members inform their partners in advance of the purpose and steps involved with the time-out.

3. Review "Time-out Information for Partners." Be prepared for the group discussion in which the group members protest that their partners will never put up with a time-out. It is important to empathize with this concern because, in many cases, it is legitimate. Emphasize that we are offering approaches which are not guaranteed to work, but which simply decrease the probability of an explosion.

4. Review "When Your Partner Blocks Your Path." One of the group members (or group leaders) should stand near the doorway, blocking the group members' path out of the room. Explain to them that their job, if they are ever blocked from being able to exit by their partner in an explosive situation, is to find a way out without "putting hands on." This is a very controversial subject. The group members (particularly men who have been charged with domestic violence) will often loudly complain—in some cases, rightfully so—that they don't have any good options in this situation. Our job here is to empathize with the difficulty of being in this position while strategizing the least dangerous and destructive ways to get out of it. It is essential to remind the group members that all of these strategies contain significant risks, but that the alternative—violence between intimate partners—is worse.

TIME-OUT

Handout

The time-out is an emergency strategy to prevent dangerous escalation of conflicts. It should *only* be used in crisis—and as you learn better communication and self-management skills, it may never have to be used at all. But you must know how to use it effectively.

If you use a time-out frequently, something is seriously wrong with your relationship. Do not use time-out simply because you wish to avoid talking about a certain subject. This is for emergencies only, and you must be prepared to resume the discussion later on.

Time-out should not be used as a weapon against the other person. It should not be used as a way of avoiding conflicts. It should not be used as a way of making the other person feel abandoned (*"I'm outta here, babe—I'll show you who's in charge!"*). Instead, time-out should be used as a sign of respect for the relationship. The message is this: *"I care enough about us that I don't want any more damage to this relationship."*

It is essential that your partner understand this message of respect. It is your job to clearly explain this in advance—and to follow it up by your actions when using the time-out correctly.

1. *"I'm beginning to feel like things are getting out of control."*

2. *"And I don't want to do anything that would mess up our relationship."*

3. *"So I need to take a time-out."*

4. *"I'm going out for a walk around the neighborhood (or to my sister's house, or the gym, etc.)."*

5. *"I'll be back in (five minutes or one hour, etc.)."*

6. *"And let's try talking about this again when I get back. OK?"* (Partner responds)

7. *"OK. Time-out."*

If he or she does not acknowledge the above statements, begin the time-out anyway—*without* making any physical contact or threats!

Leave silently—no door slamming.

While you are away from home, don't drink or use drugs or drive if your temper is out of control.

Try using "self-talk" to help you keep this in perspective:

"I'm getting upset, but I don't have to lose my cool!"

"I'm frustrated, but I don't have to control anybody else or always get my way."

"I can calm myself and think through this situation."

"I've got to think about what will be most important for the future."

Do something physical (walking, playing sports, working out, etc.) if it will help you discharge tension. Try distracting yourself with any activity that temporarily takes your mind off the intensity of the argument. Do not drink or use drugs during this time-out!

You must come back when you said you would, or call and check in. When you come back, decide together if you want to continue the discussion. Here are the options at this point:

- **Discuss it now**: This is usually the best and most respectful action, but there are some exceptions.
- **Drop the issue**: Maybe you both realize now that it was really not that big a deal.
- **Put the issue on hold**: This may be important to discuss, but it would be better to do it at later time. So long as *both* parties agree, this can work.

Each person has the right to say "no" to further discussion at that time and to suggest a time for discussion. If anger escalates again, take another time-out.

TIME-OUT INFORMATION FOR PARTNERS*

Handout

If you are still together with your partner, please bring home this information and share it with her. We have found it especially valuable for both of you to review this handout together. We recommend that she sign it to indicate that she has read and understands it. If your partner does not want to read this, or does not want to sign this, DO NOT PRESSURE HER. This will not affect how we view your success here in any way. This form is just here to provide more guidelines for all parties involved.

Please note that this section is written as if males are taking the time-outs and females have questions about what to do. **These same instructions can and should apply in any combination of partner violence, including male-to-female, female-to-male, straight or gay.** Please change the pronouns to fit your personal situation, if appropriate.

1. **How do time-outs help solve family problems?** Your partner's use of time-outs will prevent him from escalating into physical or psychological abuse. Time-outs alone do not solve destructive conflicts, but if used faithfully they will help him avoid extremely destructive behavior. Family problems have to be discussed and solutions agreed upon. This cannot happen if one person is abusive of the other. No communication takes place when there is abuse. Time-outs are a necessary first step to communicating respectfully.

2. **What do I do if every time I want to discuss an important topic with my partner, he says he is taking a time-out?** Let him take the time-out anyway. If he becomes angry and abusive, you will not be able to talk about the problems. At first he may take time-outs a lot. Just remind yourself that it is only one step and that he will be expected to use other approaches as well. Read the "Time-out" instructions—it will help you understand how the time-out situation works.

3. **What if he refuses to discuss the matter even after the time-out?** Notice in the "Time-out" instructions that he has several choices as to what he does after a time-out. He is not supposed to drop issues if they are important to you. However, he may put them on hold until he is able to both speak calmly and *listen to you*. If he refuses to discuss an issue, your insistence will *not* bring about the communication. Let him know that you are still interested in talking about the issue, but be willing to set a later time when he can be calmer when discussing it.

4. **Should I remind my partner to take a time-out when he is getting angry or abusive?** *No*. He is responsible for identifying his own feelings and taking the time-out. As long as you do it for him, he is *not* doing his job. If you are upset about his abuse, you take a time-out for yourself as long as you can do it safely. Remember, you cannot control another person's behavior; you can only protect yourself.

5. **What should I do when he takes a time-out during a discussion?** Remind yourself that this is the first step—that it is better for him to take a time-out than to be abusive toward you. Waiting for him to return can lead to your feeling frustrated or abandoned. You can use the time in a time-out for yourself and then go about your regular business.

6. **Would time-outs be useful for me?** Yes, if you find your own anger rising, a time-out is a tool you can use to calm down before you go further in working out a conflict. However, your using time-outs for yourself will not necessarily change your partner's behaviors. Time-outs are good for you to use when you are in conflicts with your children or with other people.

---

*Adapted with permission from Schechter & Ganley (1995).

WHEN YOUR PARTNER BLOCKS YOUR PATH

 **Handout**

Sometimes, your partner will not cooperate with your attempts to take a time-out, no matter how respectfully you declare one. Here is a sequence that sometimes will occur:

1. You declare a time-out (following the steps correctly).

2. Your partner blocks your path so you cannot leave.

3. Now you should remind him or her of the time-out agreement that you previously discussed.

4. But he or she continues to block the exit.

5. This is the time to offer *your partner* the opportunity to leave instead, so she does not feel abandoned. For example, you might say something like this: "OK, if you want to leave, that's cool too. I don't want you to feel like I'm leaving you. We just need a break right now until things calm down."

In this situation, you cannot afford to place any hands on your partner or to use any significant force to move her. Not only is this dangerous, but it is very likely that you will be arrested.

If none of these strategies is successful in separating the two of you, there are three basic options available to the offender:

1. Physical Escape
   - Retreat through another exit (into a bathroom or a bedroom) and lock the door.
   - Escape through a window if it is safe to do so.
   - Agree to stay and discuss the situation until your partner relaxes and no longer blocks the door, then escape.

2. Call for Help
   - Dial 911. Explain that your partner will not allow you to leave the premises. Make it clear that you are trying to avoid violence.
   - Call someone who can talk to your partner and try to calm her down to cooperate with the time-out.

3. Stay Put
   - Sit down and stay quiet. Repeat self-talk to yourself such as, "It's not worth it to get into a fight" or "It's my job to stay calm now." Use relaxation techniques, like deep breathing, to help you stay calm.

None of these options is particularly great. They all contain significant risks, but they are designed to accomplish the most important goal in this situation: preventing both people from getting hurt. We hope that you are never in this situation, but these are important strategies to keep in mind just in case this situation arises.

MIDPOINT SESSIONS: SWITCH!

This material should be presented only when one or more group members is at approximately the midpoint of their sessions. Then the regularly scheduled group content should resume.

MATERIALS

"Switch!"

GOAL

To rehearse and integrate self-management skills.

TASKS

> *1. Practice "Switch!" with any group member who has completed half of his sessions.*

PROGRAM

1. Ask the group member who has completed approximately half of his sessions to choose a disturbing situation from the past—"*perhaps the incident that got you here*"—or any other time when he has reacted with verbal or physical aggression toward his partner or other family member. Remember that you are trying to assess the member's ability to examine personal responsibility—and new options—for abusive behavior.

2. Lead the group member through the steps of "Switch!" This is a very important opportunity to assess how well the group member is able to examine himself and integrate new ideas. General instructions should be given, such as: "*When role-playing this situation, combine all the skills you've learned so far: use relaxation skills, build up your self-esteem, challenge your 'bad rap,' and think constructively.*"

   ■ The first two steps of "Switch!" are used to **identify the problem situation** and **identify the self-talk**. The target member describes the thoughts he was having before, during, and after the problem situation.

- The next step, **determining new self-talk**, focuses on what the person would like to develop as coping self-talk. The group members should help generate "counter" self-talk.
- In **modeling the situation**, the leader demonstrates the process of switching from self-defeating to self-enhancing statements, which the target member will practice during "Switch!"
- Now the reframing begins. The target member is asked to **imagine that he is back in the problem situation**. The leader further instructs the target member to begin stating aloud the self-defeating self-talk. When the group leader gives the command, the group—in unison, very loud—yells "Switch!" and the target member inserts the new self-talk. (Note: This is meant to be entertaining—and to provide a shock to the individual's typical self-talk patterns.)
- Both **self-evaluation and group feedback** follow. Group members should give feedback initially on aspects of the self-talk reframing that were done well, followed by suggestions for improvement.

3. Have the group member briefly repeat new self-talk to help solidify the changes.

SWITCH!

Handout

1. *What went wrong?*
   a. Who was involved? When was it? Where was it? Describe exactly what was happening. Be specific and objective.
   b. Replay this like a movie. What exactly did you do and say?
   c. Other group members should help by asking questions so the "movie" is very clear.

2. *What was your self-talk?*
   a. What was your self-talk before, during, and after the situation?
   b. Freeze the frame of this movie so you can stop at different points and identify the self-talk.
   c. With the group's help, analyze the self-defeating or unproductive self-talk.

3. *What new, more productive self-talk could you have used?*
   a. What would you like to have said to yourself instead in this situation?
   b. Brainstorm with group for alternative self-talk.

4. *Self-talk "Switch!"*
   a. Put yourself back in the problem situation.
   b. Practice the old self-talk out loud.
   c. When the group calls out "Switch!," try using your productive self-talk instead.

5. *What do you think? What does the group think?*
   a. What did you do that worked well?
   b. What would you do next time to improve?

Exit/Relapse Prevention Session 1

MOST VIOLENT OR MOST DISTURBING INCIDENT

This material (and the material from Exit/Relapse Prevention Session 2) should be presented only when one or more group members are at approximately the endpoint of their sessions. Then the regularly scheduled group content should resume.

MATERIALS

None

GOAL

To review the most disturbing incident in the relationship *that the group member has committed*, so that he can recognize the impact on himself and on others.

TASKS

> 1. *Review most violent or most disturbing incident with group member who is close to terminating the group program.*
> 2. *Review affect and self-talk during incident.*

PROGRAM

1. Ask a group member who is close to terminating the group program to review, in detail, the most disturbing abusive incident in his relationship *that he has committed*. This is not necessarily the most physically injurious event, but rather the one that stands out as the most emotionally upsetting. It is also important to emphasize that there might have been other more abusive incidents in his relationship committed by his partner—but this assignment is to choose a situation when he has behaved the most abusively toward her. It is very important for the group member to describe this incident as vividly as possible, in the first person present, as if it were happening in slow motion.

2. The group member should be asked to describe, at various intervals, the following information:
   - his self-talk
   - his emotions
   - his physical state

Particularly important is his affect. Group leaders may need to say repeatedly, *"Describe how you are feeling at this point."* The goal here is to diminish as much of the original denial and minimization as possible. This is an opportunity to go into more depth with these issues—particularly with some of the new skills and information that the men now have.

3. Insist that the group member also identify the following:
   - partner's and child's self-talk
   - partner's and child's emotions
   - partner's and child's physical state

Exit/Relapse Prevention Session 2
PREVENTION PLAN

This material (and the material from Exit/Relapse Prevention Session 1) should be presented only when one or more group members is at approximately the endpoint of their sessions. Then the regularly scheduled group content should resume.

MATERIALS

"Weekly Check-in"
"Prevention Plan"

GOAL

To integrate the variety of coping skills in a rehearsal for challenging situations.

TASKS

1. *Explain theory of the "Prevention Plan."*
2. *Review basic steps of "Prevention Plan."*
3. *Guide group member who is terminating the group program through the development of "Prevention Plan."*

PROGRAM

1. Explain that the "Prevention Plan" is based on a treatment called "cue therapy," which was originally developed to treat cocaine abusers at a Veterans Center. Clinical research showed that, even though the patients were exposed to many excellent treatments, many relapsed because they could not resist the old familiar "cues" that triggered the familiar drug pattern. Cue therapy was introduced so that they could carefully rehearse exposure to these cues while practicing many alternative coping strategies.

2. Ask the terminating group member to identify a cue or trigger for his own aggression. Then guide him through each of the four coping strategies listed in the "Prevention Plan." At the completion, he should have generated one strategy from each category.

3. Now role-play the cue situation and ask the volunteer to practice each of the coping strategies. Explain that, in real situations, it is rarely practical to use all of these. However, it is valuable to be equipped with as many as possible just in case.

4. *Challenges:* Who should the men *not* talk to? (thanks to James Reavis, Psy.D. for developing this technique): Discuss how important peer groups are in maintaining new attitudes and behaviors. Ask the group to role-play "negative" influences on the terminating group member.

For example, ask the group member to role-play the following situation:

> *It's Friday after work, and you're playing basketball with some friends. The game is winding down and your friends invite you out for some beers with them.*
> *You remember that your wife planned to make dinner for the two of you tonight and she asked you to be home by 6:30. You tell the guys that you have to pass, because of these plans.*

Group members should challenge him by saying some of the following:

- *"You used to be so much fun—what's happened to you, man?"*
- *"You can't let her get away with that crap!"*
- *"Prove to her who's in charge!"*
- *"Just lie to her, man—you know how they all are!"*

The selected group member should practice his response to these challenges.

PREVENTION PLAN*

Handout

PURPOSE: To prepare you for future situations when you might be tempted to become abusive toward your partner.

CUE OR TRIGGER (What could set you off?):

COPING STRATEGIES:

1. **"Scare yourself" image—Example:** Remember the damage to your family, remember being arrested, etc. What scary image would have an impact on you?

2. **Relaxation/distraction—Example:** Deep breathing, listening to music, playing basketball, etc. What would work for you?

3. **Self-talk—Example:** "This isn't worth it," "Nobody's perfect," "I want to keep my life together." What phrase would work best for you?

4. **Friends/allies—Example:** Call a friend, crisis line, therapist, sponsor, or family member. Who would that be for you?

BEHAVIOR I DO *NOT* WANT TO ENGAGE IN (BE SPECIFIC):

_____

_____

---

*Adapted with permission from Wexler (1991b).

PART III
GROUP SESSIONS: SELF-MANAGEMENT

Session 1
THE RED FLAGS OF ANGER

MATERIALS

"Weekly Check-in"
"The Cycle of Abuse"
"The Red Flags of Anger"
"Quieting Reflex" exercise on the CD-ROM (or other similar relaxation tape)

GOAL

To teach the men basic anger education and management skills; to help the group members understand typical stages in family violence; to encourage them not to use violence toward their partners; and to explore other options.

TASKS

1. *Review "Weekly Check-in."*

2. *Review homework (from Session 26; remember that the 26 sessions are repeated for the full 52-week program, so Session 26 is the last session before starting the sequence again.).*

3. *Introduce concept of red flags.*

4. *Explain "Cycle of Abuse" concept.*

5. *Review "The Red Flags of Anger."*

6. *Encourage discussion of anger and anger management, including modeling and role-play.*

7. *Play "The Quieting Reflex" on the CD-ROM.*

8. *Assign homework.*

PROGRAM

1. Present the handout "Cycle of Abuse." The handout focuses on the three primary stages in the cycle of family violence: (1) tension-building (escalation); (2) violence (explosion); and (3) calm, loving (honeymoon). Explain to the men that

this cycle is an accurate description of the patterns in *some* couples where abuse takes place. (It is particularly helpful when working with women who have been abused, because it helps them see the patterns of behavior more clearly.) However, not all couples follow this pattern. It is not inevitable that abusive behavior escalates in frequency and intensity, as the original model suggested. And not all men perceive this pattern as being the most accurate description of their own behavior. It is better to address these issues up front to deflect resistance to this model.

  a. First, present an overview of the three stages and ask the group members if they recognize some of the signs from each stage.

  b. Next, discuss the tension-building stage. Generate admission about the cues and triggers that are likely to provoke the escalation. You will be leading a group discussion about the *red flags* that trigger this escalation in the next section of this session.

  c. Discuss the honeymoon phase. Here, the tables often turn, and the person who has been so domineering becomes very dependent. The abusive person recognizes how much he needs the partner and may often cling desperately. This stage can be extremely difficult for the partner to resist, because the vulnerable emotions are so appealing. In keeping with the basic principles of behavioral psychology, both partners may feel "reinforced" by the explosion. They may come to believe (unconsciously) that **this state can only be achieved in the aftermath of violence.**

2. Introduce the concept of *red flags.* Go over the handout "The Red Flags of Anger." Explain how important it is to identify the warning signs of anger. Remind the group members that the more they know about themselves, the more "true power" they have over their own behavior. Refer to Commandment 5.

    Physical red flags: muscle tension, accelerated heartbeat, disorientation (*"What are the indicators in your body that let you know you are starting to climb the escalation ladder?"*)

    Verbal red flags: words from other people that stir things up. (*What are the key phrases or words that can make you "see red?" Weak? Stupid? Punk? Threats to leave or be unfaithful? Insults about your family?*)

    Situational red flags: paying bills, hearing certain questions, dealing with kids after having a few drinks? (*"What are the situations that are almost sure to start an argument between you and your wife or girlfriend? When you know what these are, you can plan a whole lot better—either by avoiding some of them, or by being extra careful to monitor your own behavior"*).

    Self-talk red flags: Discuss Dutton's "bitch tape" (1998). Dutton's research found that abusive men identified self-talk like *"What a bitch!"* or *"I can't believe I have to put up with such a bitch!"* as narrative triggers for abusive behavior. Ask the group members to identify their own "bitch tapes."

    "She's trying to make a fool of me."
    "She doesn't love me anymore."
    "She doesn't respect me."

3. Ask each group member to role-play a personal situation including all of the above types of red flags: physical, verbal, situations, self-talk. Make sure the other group members are genuinely convinced that they can "see" the red flags.

4. Offer these instructions for the relaxation CD-ROM:

The goal of this relaxation exercise is to give you even more tools for managing your own reactions. We do this a lot of ways in this program: self-talk, problem solving, communication skills. And this is another way for you to be in charge.

Some of you may have already learned some of these skills, which is great. Use what you already know. Just follow along with the instructions on the CD and give it your best shot.

We do not intend for you to fall asleep. If you sleep, you will not develop true relaxation skills. Feel free, however, to let your mind go in whatever direction it wants during these experiences.

5. Play the 10-minute clip on the CD, *The Quieting Reflex* (or a similar relaxation tape). Then discuss problems they might have had; for example, falling asleep or not wanting to keep their eyes closed. Discuss other forms of relaxation that they might use, such as jogging or meditation.

THE CYCLE OF ABUSE

 Handout

The Cycle of Abuse

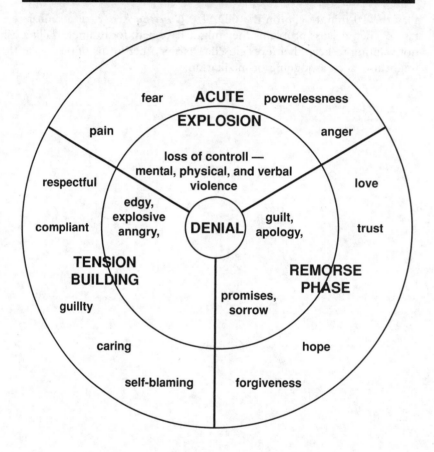

*Based on ideas from Walker (1984)

THE CYCLE OF ABUSE (con't)

 Handout

DENIAL

Denial works in each stage of the cycle to keep the cycle going. Only by breaking through this denial can the cycle be broken.

TENSION BUILDING

Tension is denied or excused as resulting from outside stress (e.g., work, etc.), or it is denied that the tension will worsen; victim blames self for own behavior. Responsibility for actions is denied by blaming the tension on partner, work, the traffic, or drinking.

EXPLOSION

The victim denies injury saying, "It is no big deal," "I bruise easily," "It didn't require police or medical help;" blames it on drinking; says the partner "didn't know what he was doing;" does not label it rape because it was her husband.

   The abuser blames the explosion on the partner, stress, etc.; believes the other person "had it coming."

REMORSE PHASE

The victim minimizes injuries by saying, "It could have been worse;" believes partner's promises that it won't happen again.

THE RED FLAGS OF ANGER

 Handout

Anger by itself is not a problem. It is a normal human emotion.

Anger is only a problem if you have too much of it, and it's with you all the time. Maybe you get headaches or can't sleep. Maybe your mind is always working on the situations that have upset you so much.

The other way, of course, that anger is a problem is if it leads to problem behaviors: verbal aggression, physical aggression, emotional withdrawal, seeking revenge, or interference with your work performance.

It is helpful to think of anger as a "secondary emotion." It is always triggered by some other emotion, frustration, extreme stress, feeling put-down, or fearing rejection. You will be hearing a lot about anger in this program, and we will be asking you to identify the primary emotion that came just before the anger.

YOUR RED FLAGS

It is very important to anticipate anger and to recognize it when it's building up. We call these signals "red flags." Here are the four different categories of red flags:

> **Physical red flags:** muscle tension, accelerated heartbeat, rush of energy, disorientation.
> **Verbal red flags:** words that stir things up. What are the key phrases or words that can make you "see red?" *Weak? Scared? Stupid? Insults about your family?*
> **Situational red flags:** paying bills, hearing certain questions, dealing with kids after having a few drinks, etc.
> **Self-talk red flags:**
> *"She's trying to make a fool of me."*
> *"She doesn't love me anymore."*
> *"She doesn't respect me."*

THE VALUE OF ANGER

Don't forget that anger can actually work to your advantage. Anger can:

- be a "cue" that something is bothering you and that you need to take care of the situation assertively;
- motivate you to work harder or prove someone's judgment about you is wrong;
- help you understand your own emotions and the emotions of others.

HOMEWORK

Handout

Write down three red flag situations that have led you to be aggressive in the past.

1.

2.

3.

Session 2
SELF-TALK AND PERSONAL STORIES

MATERIALS

"Weekly Check-in"
"Bad Rap"
"Bad Rap Quiz"
"Brief Quieting Reflex" exercise on the CD-ROM (or a similar relaxation tape)

GOALS

To introduce group members to the basic concept of self-talk and to increase aware-ness of how interpretations of events can determine feelings and reactions.

TASKS

1. *Review Weekly Check-in.*
2. *Review homework.*
3. *Explain concept of self-talk through ABCDE model.*
4. *Explain and discuss categories of "Bad Rap."*
5. *Conduct "Bad Rap Quiz."*
6. *Practice relaxation training by playing "Brief Quieting Reflex" on CD.*
7. *Assign homework.*

PROGRAM

1. Introduce a basic working model of "self-talk." Use the ABCDE model (explained below), emphasizing how the way we interpret events can determine the way we feel and act (Wexler, 1991a).

    a. **Objective event:** This is the initial event. Your wife or girlfriend comes home and says, *"I hate my job!"*

    b. **Self-talk**: You might say to yourself: *"She's trying to tell me that she doesn't want to work and that I should be making more money so she shouldn't have to!"*

    c. **Feelings and behavior**: If you interpreted it this way, you would probably feel critical of her, or act defensive, or sulk, or worry. Maybe you would say to her: *"Quit complaining! You think you're the only one who has it tough?"*

    d. **New self-talk**: Maybe there was another way to interpret what she said. Maybe she was just tired and needed some support, like we all do. Maybe it was not intended as a message or critical comment. You might be saying to yourself, *"She sounds like she's had a rotten day. What can I do to help?"*

    e. **New feelings and behavior**: If you interpreted it this way, you might say: *"Let's talk about it."* Or you might try to cheer her up. Or you might just whisk the kids off into another room and let her be alone for a while. Your response would be based on what you thought she might need, rather than defending yourself against a perceived attack.

2. Now explain the seven categories of "Bad Rap." Teach the names of the categories and go through the different examples. Ask the group members to come up with examples of their own.

3. Quiz group members with the "Bad Rap Quiz" to make sure that they get the idea. Try turning this into a *Family Feud* contest, with different teams competing for the right answer. If one team identifies the correct category for the statement, award a point. This team then has the opportunity to rephrase the statement so that it reflects "productive" or "realistic" self-talk, worth an additional point. If a team answers incorrectly, the other team can try, until one of the teams gets it right. Make sure that they learn how to revise the "faulty" self-talk into sentences that would be more "realistic" self-talk.

    This is designed to be entertaining and engaging, with one primary purpose. This purpose should be repeated and emphasized throughout this session and others:

    We want you to see how powerful your self-talk is in determining your emotions and your behaviors in any situation. And we want you to see that it is possible, in a lot of these situations, to change the self-talk and end up with emotions and behaviors that do not mess you up so much. This is another example of making you powerful— not over others, but over yourself.

4. Practice relaxation training by playing *Brief Quieting Reflex* on the CD (or a similar relaxation tape).

BAD RAP*

Handout

1. **Black and white:** Seeing things as all or nothing. Beware of words like *never, always, nothing,* and *everyone.*

   "Real men don't admit their mistakes."
   "You're either on my side or you're not."
   "You can't trust anyone over 30."

2. **Minimizing:** Downplaying your achievements.

   "Even though I finally made supervisor, it's no big deal."
   "I did well, but so did a lot of other people."
   "My counselor just gives me good feedback because she's paid to say it."

3. **Mind reading:** Assuming that others think something without checking it out.

   "I know my boss hates me—he gave me a dirty look."
   "She's avoiding me—she must be pretty mad."
   "My girlfriend didn't call me today—she must not care about me."

4. **Awfulizing:** Predicting that things will turn out "awful" for you.

   "My boss will never trust me again."
   "I know I'm not going to make it through this place."
   "Wow, he is so good at that—I'll never be able to do it that well!"

5. **Error in blaming:** Unfairly blaming yourself—or others.

   "It's all my fault," or *"It's all their fault."*
   "It's my fault my son is shy."
   "You always mess everything up for me."

6. **Down-putting:** Making too much of your mistakes (opposite of **minimizing**).

   "I failed this test; I must be dumb."
   "I'm in counseling; there must be something really wrong with me."
   "She doesn't like me; I must be ugly."

7. **Emotional reasoning:** Concluding that if you feel a certain way about yourself, then it must be true.

   "Since I feel bad about myself, I must be a bad person."
   "I feel rejected, so everybody must be rejecting me."
   "Since I feel guilty, I must have done something wrong."

---

*Adapted with permission from Wexler (1991b)

BAD RAP QUIZ*

 **Handout**

1. The counselor told me I'm doing better, but I know he tells that to everybody. (2)
2. Ever since Linda hurt me, I know redheads can't be trusted. (1)
3. Nothing's ever going to work out for me. (4)
4. It's your fault we never do anything fun. (5)
5. My parents got divorced; it must have been something about me. (5)
6. I sometimes don't get things right, so I must be lazy or stupid. (6)
7. I feel lonely, so I guess nobody likes me. (7)
8. That supervisor shows me no respect; nobody in this organization cares a damn about me. (1)

---

*The numbers in parentheses above are the "correct" answers, and correspond to the seven "Bad Rap" categories on the previous page, although group members may make a good case for other answers. Adapted with permission from Wexler (1991b).

HOMEWORK

 **Handout**

Record three examples of "bad rap" over the next week. Write down the self-talk, the category of "bad rap," and new self-talk that would have been more realistic or productive.

1. **Self-talk**

2. **Category**

3. **New self-talk**

---

1. **Self-talk**

2. **Category**

3. **New self-talk**

---

1. **Self-talk**

2. **Category**

3. **New self-talk**

Session 3

SELF-TALK AND SELF-ESTEEM

MATERIALS

"Weekly Check-in"
"House of Self-worth and Empowerment"

GOAL

To offer the group members ways of changing self-esteem through self-awareness, cognitive restructuring, or lifestyle modification.

TASKS

1. *Review "Weekly Check-in."*
2. *Review homework.*
3. *Conduct exercise "What's the Worst You Call Yourself?"*
4. *Discuss "House of Self-worth and Empowerment."*
5. *Ask group members to say something positive about themselves.*
6. *Play "Brief Quieting Reflex" on CD.*
7. *Assign homework.*

PROGRAM

1. *"What's the worst name you call yourself?"*: People often react strongly to criticism because they are already strongly criticizing themselves. By being more aware of the worst things we call ourselves or fear that someone else might call us, we can deflect the impact of the criticism.

   Explain that by talking about "weak spots" in ourselves or ways we put ourselves down, we can begin to make sense of what is happening to us. Sometimes we take in what was said about us as kids and totally believe it. Talking about it helps us to distance ourselves from it, and realize that as adults we are not so likely to be hurt as when we were kids.

71

2. Ask the men to share some of the ways they put themselves down with labels, for example: *"I'm stupid," "I'm a screw-up," "I'm just lazy."* Caution them not to reveal more than they feel comfortable revealing. Ask if they know when someone else might have called them that name. Ask if they are willing to tell what they would fear being called by someone else.

3. Reinforce the importance of positive self-esteem and talk about how self-esteem can be changed. Discuss the "House of Self-worth and Empowerment" by drawing the house on the board, much like the "House of Abuse" from New Member Session 1. Ask the group members to generate information about areas of their lives that are important to them and that provide them with experiences of self-worth. As with the "House of Abuse," the specific ideas should be clustered into different rooms of the house. Although these room names can be altered according to the particular group, suggested room names are the following:

   - Job
   - Social life
   - Relaxation
   - Parenting
   - Spirituality
   - Wife/partner relationship
   - Personal skills (athletics, manual skills, intellectual abilities, etc.)
   - Personal integrity (examples of "doing the right thing")

   Then start asking the questions:

   - *"How does it feel to live in this house?"*
   - *"How do the rooms strengthen each other?"*
   - *"What do you need to do to make sure that these rooms are filled?"*

   And, the final question:

   - *"What do these rooms support? What is on the roof?"*

   The answer is "self-worth" and "empowerment."

4. A good group activity at this time is to have each group member say something positive about himself. This can aid the bonding process as well as build self-esteem. Discuss any unusual reactions, and be sure to check out the person's feelings about what was said about him.

5. Practice relaxation training by playing *Brief Quieting Reflex* on the CD (or a similar relaxation tape).

THE HOUSE OF SELF-WORTH AND EMPOWERMENT*

 Handout

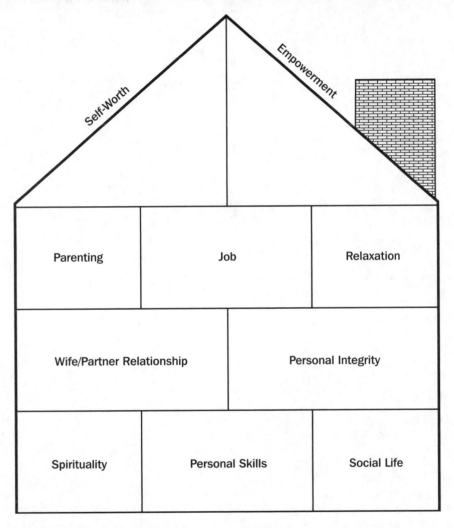

The House of Self-worth and Empowerment

Self-Worth

Empowerment

| Parenting | Job | Relaxation |

| Wife/Partner Relationship | Personal Integrity |

| Spirituality | Personal Skills | Social Life |

*The House of Abuse chart was developed by Michael F. McGrane, MSW, LICSW, Director of the Violence Prevention & Intervention Services (VPIS) of the Amherst H. Wilder Foundation, and is used here by permission. The chart is part of a complete domestic abuse curriculum entitled *Foundations for Violence-Free Living: A Step-by-Step Guide to Facilitating Men's Domestic Abuse Groups*, available from Fieldstone Alliance at 1-800-274-6024.

HOMEWORK

 **Handout**

Make a list of (1) five positive traits in yourself and (2) five personal accomplishments.

TRAITS	PERSONAL ACCOMPLISHMENTS
1.	1.
2.	2.
3.	3.
4.	4.
5.	5.

Session 4

FEELINGS AND REAL FEELINGS

MATERIALS

"Weekly Check-in"
"The Feelings List"
"Real Feelings and Core Hurts"
Men's Work *videotape: Scene II* (begin at 19:16 and end at 20:20)

GOAL

To help the group members identify a wide range of feelings and develop new ways of handling difficult ones.

TASKS

1. *Review "Weekly Check-in."*
2. *Review homework.*
3. *Discuss the "macho" role for men.*
4. *Introduce the concept of feelings.*
5. *List the four primary feelings on a board.*
6. *Review "The Feelings List."*
7. *Review "Real Feelings and Core Hurts."*
8. *Play Men's Work videotape: Scene II (begin at 19:16 and end at 20:20) and discuss.*
9. *Assign homework.*

PROGRAM

1. Many men cut themselves off from a full range of feelings because of their social-ization into a "macho" role. In general, it is difficult for men to know themselves, much less to express themselves to others. It is not the case, as many women

assume, that men do not have feelings. What happens is that the softer feelings of hurt and fear become quickly converted into anger and then into aggression. Men feel, but it isn't always obvious to themselves or to others.

Explain that men often cheat themselves by not knowing themselves fully. The tendency to hold in the "soft" emotions or to act out our "tough" ones helps to explain why men on average die seven years earlier than women. A common fear is that if men express their hurt or fear the other person will "use it against us." In a close relationship, just the opposite usually happens (thanks to Daniel G. Saunders for the preceding ideas on men's emotions).

2. Explain the following:

   Feelings are emotional states. There are four primary feelings: sadness, joy, fear (anxiety), and anger. Just as the primary colors have many shades and mixtures, so there are many shades and mixtures of feelings.

   Feelings are different from thoughts, opinions, and beliefs. "I feel you put me down" is an opinion or observation. "I felt hurt when you said that" combines a feeling statement with an observation.

3. List the four primary feelings across the top of the board. Ask the men to name similar feelings under the primary ones. With a good group discussion, you should end up with a list of 8 or 10 feeling words in each of the four categories. Point out the range of intensity in the examples given. Emphasize the importance of expressing feelings when they first arise, when then are at low intensity.

4. Review "The Feelings List." Ask a group member to pick out one of the emotions from the list—and then act it out, without any words, like charades. The rest of the group should guess the emotion. Continue on with each group member choosing a different item on the list. This should be fun, and should help the group members clarify labels for different emotions.

5. Review "Real Feelings and Core Hurts." Play the *Men's Work* CD: Scene II (begin at 19:16 end at 20:20), the vignette in which the man abuses his wife after a frustrating day at work. Ask the men to focus on the core hurts of the man in this scene and how automatically he turned these hurts into aggression, both verbal and physical.

THE FEELINGS LIST

Handout

Below is a list of some of the more common feelings. The list could go on for pages. The only way most of us (particularly men) learn about how to label our different feelings is by being around other people who give us some feedback.

For example, when you were a baby, you didn't know the names of the different colors. Someone kept telling you that the sky was blue and that the fire engine was red. You learned, after more practice, that red had many different shades: scarlet is different from pink, and maroon is not quite the same as burgundy.

The same is true for feelings. Many men feel upset inside and label it "pissed." But different levels and shades of anger may range from irritated and frustrated to furious and enraged. Furthermore, feeling "pissed" is often men's way of saying that they are really feeling hurt, threatened, or ashamed. Men's language for those feelings is usually not well developed.

- excited
- tender
- sad
- lonely
- edgy
- frustrated
- frightened
- contented
- depressed
- timid
- hurt
- jealous
- loving
- elated
- happy

See if you can classify these into one of the four major categories. Remember that there are four primary feelings: sadness, joy, fear (anxiety), and anger. Some feelings may not fit neatly into only one category.

The more familiar you are with these different feelings, the more power you have over your own experience and reactions.

Self-knowledge is power.

REAL FEELINGS AND CORE HURTS*

 **Handout**

As we have mentioned before, anger is a "secondary" emotion. It is usually preceded by a "primary" emotion that feels like a wound, attack, or anxiety.

It is extremely valuable for all of us to have the ability to label our emotions properly.

Think of a recent time when you felt angry, then try to identify the specific painful feeling you were experiencing that probably triggered it. This is called the "core hurt." Here are some examples:

- *"I felt disrespected."*
- *"I felt confused and unsure."*
- *"I felt unimportant."*
- *"I felt rejected."*
- *"I felt unlovable."*
- *"I felt powerless."*
- *"I felt ignored."*

In the future, whenever you notice anger, ask yourself this question: *"What is my real feeling and core hurt?"* If you are able to do this, you will be in a much more powerful position to truly run your own emotional and behavioral life. You will no longer be controlled by your anger.

---

*Based on ideas from Stosny (1995).

HOMEWORK

 **Handout**

Over the next week, pay attention to your feelings. Record at least one example of situation, self-talk, and description of feeling from each category of feelings: sadness, joy, fear (anxiety), anger.

1. Sadness

Situation:

Self-talk:

Description of feeling:

2. Joy

Situation:

Self-talk:

Description of feeling:

3. Fear (Anxiety)

Situation:

Self-talk:

Description of feeling:

4. Anger

Situation:

Self-talk:

Description of feeling:

Session 5
THE BROKEN MIRROR

MATERIALS

"Weekly Check-in"
Affliction *video clip (begins at 13:20 and ends at 19:25)*
"The Broken Mirror Sequence"

GOALS

To help group members understand how easily negative feelings can be activated based on the response they get from their partners or others, and how this can lead to destructive behavior.

TASKS

1. *Review "Weekly Check-in."*
2. *Review homework.*
3. *Discuss "broken mirror" concept.*
4. *Play* Affliction *video clip and review.*
5. *Review "The Broken Mirror Sequence."*
6. *Assign homework.*

PROGRAM

1. Explain the concept of the "broken mirror." A sample explanation appears on p. 82.

    The following video is from the movie Affliction; *let's watch what happens with the main character and his daughter. He has grown up with a very abusive father, and he is trying to be a better man. But he only has partial success.*
    In this scene, his 10-year-old daughter is living with his ex-wife. He has arranged for his daughter to spend the Halloween weekend with him, and he has a picture in his head of having a great time together. At some point, he has a broken

mirror experience and he doesn't handle it very well. See if you can identify what she does that leads to the broken mirror for him—and how he handles it.

2. Play the scene from *Affliction* at the Halloween party, where Jill calls her mother to pick her up because she is not having a good time (begins at 13:20 and ends at 19:25).

3. Lead a group discussion with the following questions:

   - *Describe the feeling that Wade (the father) had during the scene.*
   - *What did Jill do that broke the mirror for her father?*
   - *Did she intentionally try to make him feel bad?*
   - *What did she do to try to remind him that this did not have to be a broken mirror for him?*
   - *What did he do in response?*
   - *Do you recognize yourself in this scene?*

4. Now present "The Broken Mirror Sequence" handout. Explain that this is the way men often experience the build-up of anger and explosiveness.

THE BROKEN MIRROR SEQUENCE

 **Handout**

Each of us looks for a response from the people most important to us. Based on the response, we might feel good about ourselves or just the opposite. It's like the other person is a mirror: you look into her eyes, hear her words, watch her body language, and it's like a *good* mirror reflecting back a picture of yourself as somebody who is decent and lovable—or a *broken* mirror image of someone who is a loser. It is completely normal and human to feel this way—it happens every day to all of us.

Some people get into situations where they see broken mirrors all over the place. If your wife says she needs to work more shifts because the family needs more money, her words might be a broken mirror to you; her behavior means you are not a good enough provider.

Once a person sees (or thinks that he sees) the broken mirror, a destructive sequence often follows. The sequence goes like this:

> **Event:** Something happens in the man's life.
> **Broken mirror:** He interprets it as negative and as a statement that there is something wrong with him
> **Bad feelings:** He feels bad—but doesn't have the words or language to describe his feelings very well.
> **Emotional flooding:** The bad feelings "flood" him.
> **Taking action:** He feels the need to *do something* to make the bad feelings go away: either escape/withdraw, or retaliate against the person who (in his mind) is responsible for making him feel bad.

According to this model, when a man experiences unbearable feelings, such as hurt, shame, helplessness, fear, guilt, inadequacy, and loneliness, he frequently feels overwhelmed. So he needs to defend against these feelings, although these defenses do not provide much of a solution:

- He places blame on her and denies responsibility: *"Why do you make me feel so bad about myself?"*
- He controlls everything and everyone in the vicinity: *"I want you all to get out of your rooms and clean up this house now—or else!"*
- He uses alcohol or drugs to temporarily take away the pain.
- He seeks excitement to distract from the bad feelings: *"I'm going to go get laid by someone who really knows how to make a man feel good!"*

When these defenses provide relief, they are reinforced, and he learns to keep using them. Although, of course, some event typically triggers a reaction, he is the one who must learn to tolerate a wider range of negative emotions without acting out.

Again: If you know what you are thinking and feeling, you are in a much more powerful position to truly be in charge of your own life.

HOMEWORK

 Handout

Identify three "broken mirror" experiences over the next week. Note the situation and how this made you feel bad about yourself.

1.

2.

3.

Session 6
MASCULINITY TRAPS I

MATERIALS

"Weekly Check-in"
The Great Santini *video (high school basketball game scene: begin at 1:03:22 and end at 1:12:18)*
"Masculinity Traps"

GOAL

To increase awareness of how self-talk about "being a man" can be destructive and lead to violent behavior.

TASKS

1. *Review "Weekly Check-in."*
2. *Review homework.*
3. *Discuss concept of self-talk and "masculinity traps."*
4. *Give examples of masculinity traps.*
5. *Play* The Great Santini *video (high school basketball game scene), discuss.*
6. *Review "Masculinity Traps" and discuss.*
7. *Assign homework.*

PROGRAM

1. Explain that men engage in certain types of self-talk because of the roles in which they are placed. The primary roles, called "masculinity traps," are beliefs that men have to be in charge, must always win, and must always be "cool" and not express a range of feelings.

2. Play *The Great Santini* videotape: Scene I (begin at 1:03:22, end at 1:12:18). Discuss the ways in which the son has become oppressed by his father's warped attitudes about masculinity.

Consider these questions:

> *"Do you think Ben was more afraid of his father, or did he think that maybe his father's way was right?"*
>
> *"What options did Ben have? What could he have done differently? Could he have done anything differently without feeling "punked"?*
>
> *"What was the difference between the coach's influence and the father's influence?"*

3. Review "Masculinity Traps" handout. Encourage discussion using the following questions:

> *"Which of these masculinity traps do you recognize in yourself?"*
>
> *"Would you like your son to grow up with these masculinity traps? Why or why not?"*
>
> *"How do men suffer when they are stuck with these masculinity traps?"*
>
> *"What are some of the positive aspects of these beliefs?"*

MASCULINITY TRAPS*

 **Handout**

As you review the self-talk that represents masculinity traps, ask yourself the following questions:

1. Which of these masculinity traps do you recognize in yourself?

2. Would you like your son to grow up with these masculinity traps? Why or why not?

3. How do men suffer when they are stuck with these masculinity traps?

4. What are some of the positive aspects of these beliefs?

"I can never show my feelings. Always be tough."

> *"Never show any weakness."*
> *"Never do anything 'feminine.'"*
> *"I have to be in control at all times."*

"I must win."

> *"I must be successful at everything!"*
> *"Don't back down from a fight."*
> *"Always try to win arguments."*
> *"Be on top by finding fault in others."*
> *"Real men solve problems by force."*

"My possessions and success are the measure of who I am."

> *"My value equals my paycheck."*
> *"My car and my clothes and my house prove what kind of man I am."*

---

*Adapted with permission from Daniel G. Saunders.

HOMEWORK

Handout

As you review the self-talk that represents masculinity traps, write your answers to the following questions:

1. Which of these masculinity traps do you recognize in yourself?

2. Would you like your son to grow up with these masculinity traps? Why or why not?

3. How do men suffer when they are stuck with these masculinity traps?

4. What are some of the positive aspects of these beliefs?

Session 7
MASCULINITY TRAPS II

MATERIALS

"Weekly Check-in"
Men's Work *videotape: Scene I (begin at 2:07, end at 11:57)*
"Men Are Supposed to . . ."
Men's Work *videotape: Scene II (begin at 19:16, end at 20:20)*
Men's Work *videotape: Scene III (begin at 20:20, end at 23:42)*
"Rights as a Man"

GOAL

To increase awareness of how self-talk about "being a man" can be destructive and help develop awareness of new bystander options.

TASKS

1. Review "Weekly Check-in."
2. Review homework.
3. Play Men's Work *videotape: Scene I.*
4. Lead group members through written "Men Are Supposed to . . ." exercise.
5. Continue Men's Work *videotape: Scene II.*
6. Discuss reactions to "spaghetti" scene.
7. Play Men's Work *videotape: Scene III.*
8. Discuss self-talk and bystander issues.
9. Review "Rights as a Man."
10. Assign homework.

PROGRAM

1. Play the *Men's Work* videotape: Scene I (begin at 2:07, end at 11:57). Take a break at the point at which the exercise about "Men Are Supposed to . . ." appears on

the screen. The screen will say STOP TAPE. Ask each of the group members to fill out the "Men Are Supposed To . . ." handout. Return to the *Men's Work* videotape and listen to the examples that the actors recite. Generate a group discussion about these issues.

2. Play the *Men's Work* videotape: Scene II (begin at 19:16 and end at 20:20), the vignette in which the man abuses his wife after a frustrating day at work. Stop the tape again after the "spaghetti" scene and discuss.

   Review the self-talk of the man in this scene. **This is the most important discussion point in this entire session.** Consider alternative self-talk that he might have used and discuss the different behaviors that might have resulted.

3. Resume the *Men's Work* videotape: Scene III (begin at 20:20, end at 23:42) and watch the interaction between the two men after the "spaghetti" scene. Review reactions to the intervention from the other man. Discuss bystander issues:

   - *How does a "real man" act in situations when he observes another male behaving badly?*
   - *What options does the bystander have in these situations?*
   - *How would this change if you knew the woman personally?*
   - *What if this was your sister?*
   - *Is it an example of loyalty to ignore it?*
   - *Would it be different if you didn't like her?*

4. Review *"Rights as a Man."* Discuss ways in which it might be threatening to give up the "masculinity trap" self-talk.

MEN ARE SUPPOSED TO . . .

H a n d o u t

Men are supposed to be . . .

1.

2.

3.

4.

Men are supposed to do . . .

1.

2.

3.

4.

Men are supposed to have . . .

1.

2.

3.

4.

Men are *not* supposed to . . .

1.

2.

3.

4.

RIGHTS AS A MAN*

 Handout

1. *As a man,* I have the right to show my feelings and express my fears.

2. *As a man,* I have the right to change and the right to choose the direction of my change.

3. *As a man,* I can ask for help when I need it and offer help when I think it is needed.

4. *As a man,* I have the right to ask for what I want and the wisdom to know that I cannot always get it.

5. *As a man,* I have the right to tell people when I cannot fulfill their expectations of me.

6. *As a man,* I have the right to consider new ways of thinking, acting, and relating to people.

7. *As a man,* I am not obliged to live up to the stereotypes of how I am "supposed" to be.

8. *As a man,* I have the right to acknowledge my frustrations, disappointments, and anxieties.

9. *As a man,* I can choose to take responsibility for my actions and not allow other people's behavior to push me into choices I do not want to make.

10. *As a man,* I have the right to show my strength by choosing not to act abusively toward someone who angers me.

---

*Adapted with permission from Wachter & Boyd (1982).

HOMEWORK

 Handout

Review the "Rights as a Man" handout. Pick out three of the items and briefly describe examples from your personal history when you acted as if you had those rights.

1.

2.

3.

Session 8
JEALOUSY AND MISINTERPRETATIONS

MATERIALS

"Weekly Check-in"
"Jealousy: Taming the Green-Eyed Monster"
"Misinterpretations"

GOAL

To help men understand the ways their jealous reactions can trigger violent behavior.

TASKS

1. Review *"Weekly Check-in."*
2. Review homework.
3. Introduce concept of self-talk and jealousy.
4. Review the handout *"Jealousy."*
5. Discuss jealousy experiences.
6. Review *"Misinterpretations."*
7. Assign homework.

PROGRAM

1. One of the strongest, most consistent traits of people who act abusively in relationships is jealousy. Sometimes the jealousy is based on reality and sometimes it is entirely fantasy—stemming from the insecurity of the person or distortions based on the use of alcohol or other drugs.

2. Explain the points made in the first part of the handout "Jealousy: Taming the Green-Eyed Monster." Read the stories from the handout.

Discussion Questions

"Have you had thoughts or feelings similar to any of the people in the stories?"
"What have you found that works to reduce jealousy?"
"What constructive self-talk can you use to combat jealousy?"
"How would you respectfully ask your partner for behavior change to reduce jealousy?"

3. Review "Misinterpretations." Discuss the wide range of possible self-talk in response to the vignettes and how different outcomes and behaviors inevitably follow.

JEALOUSY: TAMING THE GREEN-EYED MONSTER*

 **Handout**

Jealousy is one of those emotions that can tie our stomach in knots in a hurry. A little bit of jealousy is natural, especially when we fear losing someone close to us. Jealousy becomes a problem when:

- we spend too much energy worrying about losing a loved one
- we let jealousy build and we try to control someone else through aggression
- we stifle a relationship by placing extreme restrictions on our partners

> *Pete* got himself really worked up whenever he went to a party with his wife, Tania. Other men were very friendly to her, and she was very friendly and outgoing herself. Pete was afraid that she would find another man more attractive and exciting than he was. He usually picked some sort of fight with her after the party, without ever telling her what he was really upset about.
>
> One day after one of these fights Pete was thinking about how upset he made himself with jealousy. He tried to look at the situation in a more objective way—the way an outside observer would. After a while he was able to say to himself: "My wife is very attractive, and it is only natural that other men will sometimes find her attractive too. That doesn't mean I'm going to lose her. She hasn't given me any reason to doubt her. My fears and anger come from doubting my self-worth. If other men like her, it only confirms what I already know—and that's positive."
>
> *Joe's* jealousy was even stronger than Pete's. He would question his girlfriend at length when she came home, asking where she had been, who she had been with, and the details of her activities. He sometimes tore himself up wondering if she was having an affair. He would get urges to follow her everywhere or demand that she stay home. It seemed that the more he questioned her, the more he disbelieved her.
>
> It was after hearing his friend talk about wanting to have an affair that Joe realized what was happening. The times when he was most suspicious of his girlfriend were the times when he was having sexual or romantic fantasies about other women. Now when he noticed jealousy, he asked himself: "Am I just thinking that she's having these fantasies because I'm feeling guilty about my own?"

For many men, mentioning jealous feelings is not a cool thing to do—to admit jealousy is to admit a weakness. If, however, jealousy is viewed as natural and as another OK emotion to share with a partner, both the man and his partner can have the privilege of getting to know you better.

> *Richard* found that the best way for him to tame the monster was to let his wife know when he felt jealous. He felt very relieved being able to talk about it. Sometimes they could laugh about it together. Instead of responding with ridicule, his wife seemed to respect him more. Both of them went on to say what behavior from each other they could and could not tolerate—such as affairs, flirting, or having friends of the opposite sex. They were able to work out some contracts that specified the limits of the relationship.

What Pete, Joe, and Richard learned about taming jealousy was the following:

1. Some jealousy is normal, and it's best to talk about it rather than hide it.
2. People can choose to see their wife's or girlfriend's attractiveness and behavior in the most negative possible way—or they can turn it around and see it in a way that is not such a threat.
3. It will help people if they ask themselves: *"Is my jealousy coming from my guilt about my own fantasies or behavior?"*
4. Men have the right to request and contract for some specific limits on their partner's behavior (not thoughts), and women have the same right.

---

*Thanks to Daniel G. Saunders for contributing these ideas.

MISINTERPRETATIONS*

Handout

Research shows that the way people think about their partner—the stories they tell themselves about the situation—plays a key role in launching abusive behavior.

The main difference has to do with what is called reading negative intent, or making "hostile interpretations." A man who has been abusive is much more likely to think that his wife's or girlfriend's behavior was *intended* to hurt and humiliate him. He cannot just attribute her behavior to the fact that she is different from him, or that she wasn't thinking, or even that she may have been insensitive in that situation.

To discuss the self-talk *about your partner's intentions,* consider the following situations:

> *You are at a social gathering and you notice that for the past half-hour your wife has been talking and laughing with an attractive man. He seems to be flirting with her.*

> *You are interested in sex and let your girlfriend know this. She isn't very interested, but agrees to have sex. You begin to start things, making romantic moves. After a little while, you notice that she isn't very responsive; she doesn't seem to be very "turned on" or interested in what you are doing.*

Men who are more likely to act abusively typically have "hostile interpretations" like these:

> *"She was trying to make me angry."*
> *"She was trying to put me down."*
> *"She was trying to power trip me."*
> *"She was trying to pick a fight."*

Other men might have more neutral or even positive interpretations like these:

> *"I wish she would spend some more time with me here; I'll go over and talk with her."*
> *"She sometimes forgets that I'm not a good mixer; I'll talk to her about what I need the next time we go out."*
> *"I'm glad she's having a good time. It's a relief to me that I don't have to take care of her in social situations."*
> *"I'm kind of disappointed, but there are plenty of reasons why she doesn't want to have sex right now—no big deal."*

---

*Based on ideas from Holtzworth-Munroe & Hutchinson (1993).

HOMEWORK

 **Handout**

1. Record three experiences of jealousy over the next week. These can include anything from high levels (like seeing your wife or partner flirting with another man) to low levels (like observing your supervisor giving approval to someone else). If you do not notice any this week, recall experiences from previous weeks.

   a.

   b.

   c.

2. Fill out "Alcohol and Other Substances Questionnaire." Prepare to discuss this in the group session next week.

Session 9

SUBSTANCE ABUSE AND RELATIONSHIP ABUSE: WHAT'S THE CONNECTION?

MATERIALS

"Weekly Check-in"
"Alcohol and Other Substances and Abuse: What's the Connection?"
"Alcohol and Other Substances Questionnaire"
"Why Do I Use?"

GOAL

To help each group member assess his own pattern of substance use or abuse and to identify the specific relationship between use of substances and relationship abuse.

TASKS

1. Review "Weekly Check-in."
2. Review first part of homework.
3. Discuss "Substance Abuse and Relationship Abuse: What's the Connection?"
4. Review "Alcohol and Other Substances Questionnaire."
5. Review and discuss "Why Do I Use?"
6. Assign homework.

PROGRAM

1. Many people who hurt the ones they love have problems with alcohol. Some also have problems with other drugs, like pot and cocaine. It is unlikely, however, that alcohol and other drugs *directly* cause aggression. Rather, the causal connection appears to be indirect, acting through people's expectations, cultural norms, personality, mind-set, and setting. And during withdrawal, the person may become irritable and liable to lash out. Long-term abuse may contribute to paranoia and aggression.

Some people who are abusive have a true addiction to alcohol or other drugs. Anyone who has relatives who are alcoholics should be told to be particularly cautious about drinking. It may be best to abstain from alcohol entirely. Blackouts are one sign of severe alcohol abuse. The group members need to be made aware that, while drinking heavily, they may seriously hurt a loved one or a stranger and never remember the event. Society can still hold them responsible for their behavior while drunk, because they put themselves at risk by taking the first drink.

2. Review "Alcohol and Other Substances and Abuse: What's the Connection?" and discuss.

3. Review "Alcohol and Other Substances Questionnaire" and discuss.

4. Review and discuss "Why Do I Use?"

SUBSTANCE ABUSE AND RELATIONSHIP ABUSE: WHAT'S THE CONNECTION?*

 **Handout**

Some people who hurt the ones they love have problems with alcohol. Some also have problems with other drugs, like pot or cocaine. Ours is a culture that often encourages the abuse of alcohol and the display of aggression under this influence. People under the influence sometimes do things impulsively that they might not ordinarily do, and their judgment and control are impaired.

People use chemicals for many different reasons. On the questionnaires that follow, think about the reasons you use alcohol or drugs. Then, identify whether alcohol or other drugs impair your judgment or cause you to become aggressive. Many people identify these themes as they think about these issues:

1. **Social drinking.** There may be peer pressure or cultural pressure to abuse alcohol. Commercials even emphasize "Why ask 'Why?' Have another beer."

2. **Habit.** Many people think that socializing is only fun with alcohol use. Others believe the only way to unwind is through drinking. Drinking becomes routine.

3. **Psychological dependency.** When alcohol use is well established, it's hard to imagine doing without it. By this stage, people have usually tried to stop—but there are too many reasons to keep using.

4. **Physical dependency.** Once the person is physically addicted, withdrawal can have severe effects.

Ask yourself these questions as you think about the ways in which drugs or alcohol may be affecting your relationship problems.

> *"Have you ever tried to cut back on your drinking or drug use?"*
> *"Has anyone ever been annoyed about your drinking or told you that you have a substance problem?"*
> *"Have you ever felt guilty for anything you've done under the influence?"*
> *"Have you ever experienced memory lapses or 'blackouts'" ?*

Any "yes" answers indicate that alcohol use has probably impaired your ability to be fully in control of your life. Remember the 100% rule regarding responsibility. Alcohol problems are progressive—without help, they get worse. Can you really be 100% committed to being in control of your life and still continue to use alcohol or drugs?

---

*Adapted with permission from Daniel G. Saunders, Ph.D., unpublished.

ALCOHOL AND OTHER SUBSTANCES QUESTIONNAIRE

Handout

1. How often do you use alcohol or other drugs?
   a. Never
   b. Once every few months
   c. At least once a month
   d. At least once a week
   e. A few times a week
   f. Every day

2. What are the main reasons that you use alcohol or drugs?
   a.

   b.

   c.

3. What are the main "cues" for drinking or using drugs?
   a. Which people?

   b. What places/life events/situations (parties, work stress, sports games, etc.)?

   c. What emotions (sadness, anger, celebration, etc.)?

   d. What self-talk ("This isn't fair," "I deserve this," "It's time to have fun," "Nobody can control me," etc.)

4. Name one time when you became more abusive or aggressive when using alcohol or drugs.

5. Has anyone ever told you that your alcohol or drug use is a problem?

WHY DO I USE?

 **Handout**

Think about the reasons why you use (or abuse) alcohol or other substances. Even if your use does not cause many problems in your life, it still serves some purpose. Check off on the list below the different reasons for your alcohol use or use of other substances.

_____	To relax
_____	To feel more at ease in social situations
_____	Just because it tastes good
_____	Because my friends expect me to
_____	To have fun
_____	To avoid other people
_____	To feel more relaxed about having sex
_____	To avoid bad feelings (anger, depression, anxiety, loneliness, etc.)
_____	To have an excuse for getting rowdy
_____	To feel better about myself
_____	To stop worrying about problems
_____	To get a little buzzed
_____	To get really drunk
_____	To go to sleep

HOMEWORK

 **Handout**

Just for one week, keep track of how much alcohol you consume. Make note of the day, the time of day, the situation, and the number of drinks. Remember that "one drink" is defined as one 6 oz glass of wine, one 12 oz beer, or 1½ oz hard liquor.

Session 10
ACCOUNTABILITY

MATERIALS

"Weekly Check-in"
"Accountability Defenses"
"Accountability Statement"

GOAL

To help the group members gain as clear an understanding as possible of their own destructive behaviors and the rationalizations they have used to justify them.

TASKS

1. *Review "Weekly Check-in."*
2. *Review homework.*
3. *Review "Accountability Defenses."*
4. *Review "Accountability Statement" in detail with each group member.*
5. *Assign homework.*

PROGRAM

1. Review "Accountability Defenses" and spend some time discussing individual answers. Make sure that all group members clearly understand each of the defenses and specifically identify some of their own.

2. Introduce the "Accountability Statement." Review each line carefully. Assist the men in filling out their own form using group discussion. In this structured discussion, each group member should be able to identify specific ways in which he has acted destructively in his primary relationship. This is purposely structured so that *anyone* could identify incidents that would fit this description. We are hoping to create a nondefensive atmosphere in which the men can openly recognize their abusive behaviors and clearly identify the ways in which at that particular time they justified them.

If you have background information on the incident history, either from the men's previous reports or from previous documentation, it can be helpful to "remind" them of examples of behavior destructive to the relationship. This review is designed to give the men time to examine their behavior and self-talk in some detail and to generate group discussion about the rationalization process. Refer to Commandment 1 (*We are all 100% responsible for our own behavior*) throughout this discussion.

ACCOUNTABILITY DEFENSES

Handout

Most people who behave destructively toward their partner find a way to justify it in their own minds. Even though they do not usually believe in being abusive toward a family member or partner, in certain situations they "make an exception."

Then, afterwards, they figure out some way to make it OK, rather than simply saying the obvious: "I blew it. I crossed over a line, and it's nobody's fault but my own."

Here are some typical examples. Circle any that you have used and write in the specific words that you have said to yourself or others:

No big deal: *"I wasn't violent; all I did was slap her."*

Intention: *"I didn't mean to hurt her—I just wanted her to understand!"*

Self-expression: *"It was my turn to let her know what I've been going through!"*

Intoxication/loss of control: *"I was drunk; what can I say?"/"I just flipped out; I didn't even know what I was doing."*

Projection of blame: *"It's her fault; if she hadn't pushed me, or nagged me, or spent too much money . . ."*

Distortion of role: *"I had to get physical with her for her own good—she was acting so crazy!"*

ACCOUNTABILITY STATEMENT*

 **Handout**

We are making an assumption here—that all of you want the best in your relationship and do not want to be in an abusive or destructive relationship. But something seems to come along and bring out behaviors in you that you thought you would never find yourself doing.

But we are all still accountable for our own actions.

To be accountable means to acknowledge and take responsibility for your actions. This handout will help you acknowledge destructive behavior in relationships. Although such behavior does not always turn into physical abuse, practically everyone—in almost *all* emotionally intimate relationships—behaves destructively at times. This is an opportunity to assess ways in which you recognize past mistakes and can demonstrate a desire to change them.

As you fill out this form, remember Commandment 1: "We are all 100% responsible for our own actions." This form will not be turned in, but will be used in the group discussion.

We are not asking you to admit to something that you did not do, or to take responsibility for something that someone else has done.

"*I have acted destructively toward my partner in the following ways.*" (circle each):

Verbal abuse	Controlling partner	Intimidation	Mind games
Property destruction	Manipulating kids	Threats	Forced sex
Put-downs	Stalking	Monitoring	Sexual put-downs
Isolation of partner	Controlling $	Mail/phones	Affairs
Physical restraint	Pushing	Ignoring/withdrawal	Kicking
Throwing things	Choking	Slapping	Other
		Use of weapons	

Other: _____

- "*I take responsibility for these destructive behaviors. My behavior was not caused by my partner. I had a choice.*"

- "*I have used the following to rationalize my destructive behaviors in this relationship (e.g., alcohol, stress, anger, "she was nagging me," etc.).*"

1.

2.

3.

- "*I recognize that my partner may be distrustful, intimidated, and fearful of me because of these behaviors.*"

---

*Adapted with permission from Pence & Paymar (1993).

HOMEWORK

Handout

Over the next week, pay attention to your self-talk and behaviors. Identify two examples in which you blamed someone else for your feelings or behaviors. Examples from the past may be used if none occurs to you this week.

1.

2.

Session 11
PUT-DOWNS FROM PARENTS

MATERIALS

"Weekly Check-in"
"Put-downs from Parents"
The Great Santini *video (one-on-one basketball scene: begin at 31:48, end at 40:23).*

GOAL

To help the men recognize how their own childhood experiences of shame or humiliation may put them more at risk for acting abusively in their adult relationships.

TASKS

1. *Review "Weekly Check-in."*
2. *Review homework.*
3. *Introduce concept of put-downs from parents.*
4. *Play* The Great Santini *video (one-on-one basketball scene: begin at 31:48, end at 40:23) and discuss.*
5. *Have group members fill out the "Put-Downs From Parents" questionnaire, then discuss.*
6. *Assign homework.*

PROGRAM

1. Before presenting the video, present some basic ideas from Dutton's research about the relationship between male shame and domestic violence (Dutton, with Golant, 1995; Dutton, van Ginkel, & Strazomski, 1995).

   This research showed that the recollections of assaultive males were characterized by memories of rejecting, cold, and abusive fathers. In analysis after analysis, the scales measuring rejection were more important in influencing future abusiveness than those measuring physical abuse in childhood alone. The research showed that abusive men have frequently experienced childhoods characterized by humiliation, embarrassment, shame, and global attacks on their sense of self. Their parents would often publicly humiliate them or punish them at random.

Typical shaming comments include the following:

- *"You're no good."*
- *"You'll never amount to anything."*
- *"I should have had an abortion."*
- *"It's your fault that my life is a mess."*

People who have been exposed to shame will do *anything* to avoid it in the future. They blame others for their behavior. The result is a man who sometimes needs affection but cannot ask for it, is sometimes vulnerable but can't admit it, and is often hurt by some small symbol of lack of love but can only criticize.

When males have been rejected and shamed by their fathers, they become hypersensitive to situations that *might* be interpreted as shame situations in the future. So they are quicker to experience shame, and quicker to feel that they have to *do something* immediately to wipe it out. In these cases, men often blame their partners for making them feel this shame or humiliation, and they turn their rage on their partners to regain some sense of self. If it happens repeatedly with more than one woman, men may go from blaming her to blaming "them."

2. In presenting these ideas, try to use the word *put-down* rather than *shame* or *humiliation*. The word *shame* is likely to lead to defensiveness and denial, and the word *put-down* can be interchanged to present the same ideas.

3. Play *The Great Santini* video (begin at 31:48, end at 40:23). Discuss the ways in which the father relentlessly attempts to humiliate his son because of his own insecurities. Guide the group discussion with the following questions:

- *"How does Ben feel in this situation?"*
- *"Would you want your son to feel like this?"*
- *"What was the intention of the Great Santini's actions? Was he trying to humiliate his son? Or was he trying to bring out the highest level of excellence, in a way that turned out to be destructive?"*
- *"How do you feel about the role of Ben's mother in defending her husband?"*

4. After this general discussion, ask the group members to fill out the "Put-Downs from Parents" questionnaire. **We have discovered that the men are much more forthcoming about reporting information on this questionnaire after watching this video.** These scales are not to be scored. They are only intended to help stimulate memories and discussion. Ask the men if they can identify experiences similar to Ben's in the movie.

5. Make sure to point out the connection between shame experiences from the past and self-talk in the present, particularly in relationship situations. The basic formula to emphasize is that men who were shamed (particularly by their fathers) as boys are especially sensitive to possible shaming situations as adults. So they are likely to tell themselves—more frequently than others—that they are being shamed. And they are likely to feel compelled to take some action to obliterate the perceived source of the shame.

- Ask the men if they can identify ways in which they may be hypersensitive to criticism or put-downs because of their experiences as children.
- Ask them what kind of self-talk they can use next time they notice this type of situation.

PUT-DOWNS FROM PARENTS*

 Handout

Please write in the number listed below (1–4) that best describes how often a put-down experience happened to you with your mother (or stepmother, female guardian, etc.) and father (or stepfather, male guardian, etc.) when you were growing up. If you had more than one mother/father figure, please answer for the persons whom you feel played the most important role in your upbringing.

   You might choose to share your responses with the group but that decision is yours alone. The more honest you can be as you describe yourself and your history, the more you will be able to benefit from this program.

1	2	3	4
Never	Occasionally	Often	Very Frequently

	Father	Mother
1. *"I think that my parent wished I had been a really different kind of child."*	_____	_____
2. *"As a child, I was physically punished or scolded in the presence of others."*	_____	_____
3. *"I was treated as the "scapegoat" of the family."*	_____	_____
4. *"I felt my parent thought it was my fault when he or she was unhappy."*	_____	_____
5. *"I think my parent was mean and held grudges against me."*	_____	_____
6. *"I was punished by my parents without having done anything."*	_____	_____
7. *"My parent criticized me and/or told me how useless I was in front of others."*	_____	_____
8. *"My parent beat me for no reason."*	_____	_____
9. *"My parent would be angry with me without letting me know why."*	_____	_____

---

*Adapted with permission from Dutton, van Ginkel, & Strazomski (1995).

HOMEWORK

 **Handout**

Fill out the "Put-downs from Parents" chart again, this time from the perspective of one of your own children. If you do not have children, pick a child you know well and try to fill it out from his or her perspective.

Session 12
SHAME-O-PHOBIA

MATERIALS

"Weekly Check-in"
Good Will Hunting *video* (begin at 1:30:23, end at 1:34:52)

GOAL

To help the men recognize how their own childhood experiences of shame or humiliation may put them more at risk for acting abusively in their adult relationships.

TASKS

1. *Review "Weekly Check-in."*
2. *Review homework.*
3. *Introduce concept of "shame-o-phobia."*
4. *Play* Good Will Hunting *video and discuss.*
5. *Assign homework.*

PROGRAM

1. Introduce the term *shame-o-phobia*. This is a handy way of identifying the profound fear many men have of the possibility of feeling shamed. *Shame-o-phobia* leads to desperate attempts to avoid possibly shaming situations. It also leads to defensive and aggressive reactions to the experience of shame.

2. Introduce the *Good Will Hunting* video (begin at 1:30:23, end at 1:34:52) about personal shame. In this scene, the main character reveals to his girlfriend his childhood history of abuse and neglect. He expresses it to her in a defensive rage, and it profoundly inhibits him from forming a positive relationship with a good woman who loves him.

3. Introduce the video:

> *This movie is about a young man, played by Matt Damon, who has grown up in rough neighborhoods on the streets of South Boston. He has been in and out of foster homes, physically abused, and has run with a real rough crowd. He finally meets a woman who is actually a good match for him, but he is terrified about getting closer to her. Watch what happens in this scene when she invites him to move to California with her. Watch how his fear of being more known by her leads to aggression toward her. This is a classic example of shame-based interpersonal violence.*

4. Play the video clip and discuss. Guide the discussion with the following questions:
   - *What takes place for Will in this scene which leads him to feel shame?*
   - *Can you identify the key words from his girlfriend that seem to trigger his shame reactions (scared, not honest, "I want to help you")?*
   - *Do you think she is intending to shame him?*
   - *How does he react to the experience of shame?*
   - *How does the concept of "anticipatory shame" come into play?*
   - *Does his behavior qualify as abuse? What is the most hurtful thing he does in this scene?*
   - *Can you imagine other ways he could have handled this whole conversation? What self-talk would have been necessary for him to do this?*

HOMEWORK

 Handout

Identify one time when you felt shamed by your wife or girlfriend and describe how you handled this.

PART IV

GROUP SESSIONS: RELATIONSHIP SKILLS

Session 13
ASSERTIVENESS

MATERIALS

"Weekly Check-in"
"Assertiveness"
"What Is Assertive Behavior?"
"Keeping Track"

GOAL

To teach the men to be more assertive through self-awareness and cognitive restructuring.

TASKS

1. Review "Weekly Check-in."
2. Review homework.
3. Review "Assertiveness."
4. Discuss the four types of behavior.
5. Discuss "What Is Assertive Behavior?"
6. Model and role-play assertive behavior.
7. Discuss "Keeping Track."
8. Assign homework.

PROGRAM

Review "Assertiveness" and "What Is Assertive Behavior?" as a way of giving basic education about assertiveness and getting the men to become aware of their own degree of assertiveness.

Write the assertiveness definition on the board:

Assertiveness: Taking care of your own needs, thoughts, and feelings—in a way that is least likely to make the other person feel attacked or act defensive.

119

Refer back to this definition again and again as you review examples. In future sessions, give the group members a "pop quiz" on this definition.

While discussing the four types of behaviors in the first handout, encourage the men to give examples. The group leaders should give other examples, then model and role-play the different assertive behaviors. Encourage the men to think of benefits of assertiveness for them personally or for the relationship.

Remind the group members that these are tools, not rules. Sometimes it makes sense to be passive, and sometimes (as in self-defense situations) it even makes sense to be aggressive. These tools are all designed primarily for relationships that we *care* about—relationships that we want to preserve as respectfully as possible.

ASSERTIVENESS

 **Handout**

We all have a wide variety of ways that we handle conflicts with other people. In *The STOP Program*, we usually (but not always) recommend "assertive" communication. Here is a working definition of "assertiveness" and examples of other behavior style.

Assertiveness: Taking care of your own needs, thoughts, and feelings—in a way that is least likely to make the other person feel attacked or act defensive

1. **Assertiveness.** This behavior involves knowing what you feel and want. It also involves expressing your feelings and needs directly and honestly without violating the rights of others. At all times you are accepting responsibility for your feelings and actions.

   "It bothered me when you were late coming back from shopping, because I had to rush off to work."

2. **Aggressiveness.** This type of behavior involves attacking someone else, being controlling, provoking, and maybe even violent. Its consequences could be destructive to others as well as yourself.

   "What the hell's wrong with you? All you ever think about is yourself!"

3. **Passivity.** The person withdraws, becomes anxious, and avoids confrontation. Passive people let others think for them, make decisions for them, and tell them, what to do.

   "I feel resentful but don't express it or deal with it. I feel like it's useless: either I don't deserve any better, or nobody will ever listen to me anyway. Usually I will become depressed and believe that my partner is purposely trying to take advantage of me—but I do nothing about the situation."

4. **Passive-aggressive behavior.** In this behavior the person is not direct in relating to people, does not accept what is happening—but will retaliate in an indirect manner. This type of behavior can cause confusion. The other person feels "stung," but can't be exactly sure how or why. And the person who has done the stinging can act as though he has done nothing at all—and imply that the other person is just "too sensitive."

   "I act coldly toword my girlfriend, then pretend that nothing's wrong when she asks me about it."
   "I felt unappreciated by my wife so I "forgot" to give her a phone message, or I made some "joking" comment about her weight.

WHAT IS ASSERTIVE BEHAVIOR?*

Handout

1. Asking for what you want but not being demanding.

2. Expressing feelings.

3. Genuinely expressing feedback or compliments to others and accepting them.

4. Disagreeing, without being aggressive.

5. Asking questions and getting information from others.

6. Using "I" messages and "I feel" statements without being judgmental or blaming.

7. Making eye contact during a conversation (unless this is inappropriate in the person's culture).

EXAMPLES

1. *"Can you give me some feedback about how I handled the kids' homework tonight?"*

2. *"I feel embarrassed when you tease me about my weight in front of my friends."*

3. *"Mom, I know you want us to call more often, but I don't think you realize how busy we both are."*

4. *"Corey, I just saw your report card and I'm concerned. Let's sit down and talk about this together."*

5. *"Sarah, I'd like to talk about this later after we've both cooled off."*

6. *Look the person in the eye and say, "I really care about you, let's work this out."*

*Adapted with permission from Geffner & Mantooth (1995)

KEEPING TRACK

 Handout

Keep a record of a situation that upset you during the week. Record the information below. List the situation and date; body reactions; self-talk; how you felt; what you did; the best way to handle it.

Situation & date	
Body reactions (physical feelings)	
Self-talk	
How I felt (emotions)	
What I did	
The best way to handle it	

HOMEWORK

Handout

Record a situation that upset you during the week on the "Keeping Track" handout. As you think about it, record what you would *like* to have done in this situation.

Session 14
EXPRESSING FEELINGS AND ASKING FOR CHANGE

MATERIALS

"Weekly Check-in"
"Requests and Refusals"
"Asking for Change"
"Keeping Track"

GOAL

To teach the men specific techniques to express feelings and request change from others.

TASKS

1. *Review "Weekly Check-in."*
2. *Review homework.*
3. *Review and practice "Requests and Refusals."*
4. *Review and practice "Asking for Change."*
5. *Assign homework.*

PROGRAM

1. Explain the concept of assertive requests from the handout "Requests and Refusals." Make it clear that these requests are presented as questions, not as statements or demands. Discuss the two types of assertive requests.

2. Model and role-play assertive requests for each of the situations and discuss.

3. Explain the concept of assertive refusals from the handout "Requests and Refusals."

4. Model and role-play assertive refusals for each of the situations and discuss.

5. Review the "Asking for Change" handout. Role-play and discuss the examples. **Remind the group members that the theme here is respectful communication, which is more likely to bring about the relationship they truly want.**

REQUESTS AND REFUSALS

Handout

ASSERTIVE REQUESTS

These are presented as questions, not as statements or demands. There are two types of assertive requests:

1. Requests for changes in another person's behavior. This request is used when you would like someone to start doing something that you like—or stop doing something that you don't like.

2. Requests for verbal responses from someone else. This type is used when you would like information from someone. It is especially useful when you think that someone is pressuring you and you want clarification. Try using assertive requests for the following scenarios:

   - Ask to borrow money from a friend.
   - Ask someone in a waiting room to stop smoking because it is bothering your child.
   - Ask the lawyer you hired (whom you haven't heard from in a month) to speed up your case.
   - Ask your wife or girlfriend not to tease you any more about your weight.

ASSERTIVE REFUSALS

These are presented in a clear, respectful way. Here are some guidelines:

> Clearly state "No."
> Offer a reason for the "No." (not always needed)
> Suggest an alternative for how the other person can get his or her needs met.
> Consider offering to help—but at some other time or under other conditions.

Try using assertive refusals for the following scenarios:

   - *"Excuse me—could I borrow your car today?"*
   - *"I want to talk about this right now!"*
   - *"We're all going out for a drink after work. You used to love to party! Come on and join us—one drink won't hurt you!"*
   - *"Honey, could you help me clean out this garage today? It's such a mess."*

ASKING FOR CHANGE

Handout

"I" messages are one method to use when you want to communicate your feelings, meanings, and intentions. "I" messages are specific, nonjudgmental, and focus on you. In contrast, "you" messages are hostile, blaming, and focused on the other person. Reframing "you" messages into "I" messages can help you communicate—because the other person will not feel attacked.

Construct "I" messages by using these phrases:

1. **When you** (just describe, don't blame) . . .

2. **I feel** (state the feeling) **because** (explain in more detail) . . .

Note: Using the word *because* with an explanation can help by giving the other person more information to understand the point you are making.

3. **I wish** (specify a new behavior that you would like the other person to use instead) . . .

4. **And if you can do that, I will** (explain how the other person will benefit) . . .

The different parts of the "I" message do not have to be delivered in the same exact order. The important thing is to keep the focus on yourself and to stay away from blame.

> *"When you take long phone calls during dinner I get angry because I begin to think you don't want to talk to me. I wish you would tell whoever's calling that you'll call back because we're in the middle of dinner. And if you can do that, I'll make sure not to hassle you about being on the phone later."*

> *"When you don't come home or call I get worried that something has happened to you. I would really like you to call me if you're going to be late. And if you can do that, I promise not to have an attitude when you get home."*

> *"When you yell at me right in the middle of a busy time at work I get so rattled that I end up making more mistakes. I wish that you would lighten up when you know that I'm busy. And if you can do that, I will be a lot easier to work with."*

CLASSIC MISTAKES

1. Being too vague: *"When you are selfish . . ."*

2. Using put-downs (*"You are so controlling!"*) instead of describing a specific behavior (*"Last night it bothered me that you gave me so many instructions about the kids."*).

3. Saying *"I feel that you . . ."* instead of *"I feel (emotion)."*

4. Not offering a specific and realistic new behavior (*"I want you to become a more outgoing person."*).

KEEPING TRACK

Keep a record of a situation that upset you during the week. Record the information below.

Situation & date	
Body reactions (physical feelings)	
Self-talk	
How I felt (Emotions)	
What I did	
The best way to handle it	

HOMEWORK

 **Handout**

Record a situation that upset you during the week in the "Keeping Track" handout, and as you think about it, record what you would *like* to have done in this situation.

Session 15
HANDLING CRITICISM

MATERIALS

"Weekly Check-in"
"Handling Criticism"
"Keeping Track"

GOAL

To teach the group members specific ways of dealing with criticism effectively.

TASKS

> 1. *Review "Weekly Check-in."*
> 2. *Review homework.*
> 3. *Review the handout "Handling Criticism."*
> 4. *Model assertive responses to criticism.*
> 5. *Guide group members through role-plays of handling criticism.*
> 6. *Review "Keeping Track."*
> 7. *Assign homework.*

PROGRAM

1. In all relationships, people become critical of each other—constructively or destructively. It is difficult for most people to deal with criticism, and in most cases they get defensive. A major part of communicating effectively is not only to give constructive criticism but to receive criticism.

    The objective of this session is to teach skills in taking criticism in the most assertive, nondefensive possible fashion.

2. Give group members the handout "Handling Criticism." The opening sections, including the nonconstructive ways of dealing with criticism, can be portrayed in a humorous way. Use examples and role-play when teaching both nonconstructive and constructive ways of handling criticism.

HANDLING CRITICISM*

Handout

Every destructive and defensive response is designed to shut down the other person and the conversation. If these are your goals, then you should continue to use these responses. But if your goal is to have a more respectful relationship where both people get heard, then you may need to change.

DESTRUCTIVE AND DEFENSIVE RESPONSES

Everyone is occasionally criticized. How you handle criticism is especially important in intimate relationships. It is not uncommon to react defensively. Typical responses to criticism are the following:

Avoid the criticism or critic

Ignore the criticism, change the subject, clown around, refuse to talk about it, act busy, withdraw, or even walk away. Examples:

> When your wife says something critical to you, don't respond verbally. Just give her a look that says "go to hell"—and walk out of the room.
> When she is trying to talk to you, look at the floor, stare into space, or just look through her. Avoid making direct eye contact.
> Shut down the conversation by saying: *"I don't want to talk about this—subject closed!"*
> Suppose you are really late coming home and your wife is upset and wants to know where you have been. You could change the subject by talking about the kids.

Practice "avoiding"

Your wife says to you, *"You don't help much with the housework around here."* How would you "avoid" the criticism?

Deny the critical comment

Deny facts, argue, present evidence, do not take any responsibility for anything.

> Argue about the facts. Fight about all the minor details. For example, *"No, I never said you were fat. I just said that your dress looks tighter on you than it used to."*
> Deny that it happened. *"I wasn't drunk at the party." "I don't know what you're talking about, I don't understand."*

> Your girlfriend has made dinner for both of you. You told her you would be home at 6:30. After you come home an hour late from playing basketball, she says, *"I don't know why I bother to treat you well. You should have been home when you told me you would be!"* How would you "deny" the criticism?

Make excuses

Act very sorry but have an alibi or excuse, or make it sound like your behavior was no big deal.

> You were late to pick up your girlfriend, so you go into detail about how the keys got lost, you had to search for them, and the baby is always losing everything. Your girl friend will soon just want to forget she ever said anything.

---

*Adapted from Geffner & Mantooth (1995).

Again you are late and your girlfriend is upset. Make statements like, *"Well, so what if we didn't get to the movie on time? Look at all the important things I have to take care of everyday."*
"So I spent a lot of time talking to her at the party, that doesn't mean I care about her. I was just being friendly. You're just overreacting because you're so insecure."

You are getting phone calls from an old girlfriend and not doing anything to discourage them. Your wife says, *"You obviously care a lot more about her than you do about me. You tell her to stop calling this house!"* How would you "make excuses" about the criticism?

Fight back
Attack and get even. Put her on the defensive. This can be aggressive (direct) or passive–aggressive (indirect).

Suppose your wife says something about you not helping out enough with the baby. You can attack her for always talking to you at the wrong time or saying it in the wrong way. Or you can attack her weight, housekeeping, or handwriting. You could get even by being careless about the furniture she really cares about or being late when she really wanted to be somewhere on time.
"Why do you always bring these things up at the wrong time? Don't you know how stressed out I am?"
"Why are you always such a bitch?"
Or the extreme version of "fighting back": Grab your wife, put your hand over her mouth, threaten to hit her if she doesn't shut up.

You drove home after having too many beers. Your wife says, *"That was so stupid. Don't you even care about me or the kids?"* How would you "fight back" at the criticism?

CONSTRUCTIVE RESPONSES
As you can see, all these ways of handling criticism can seriously hurt good communication and destroy relationships. Major arguments may develop because someone has been ignored, argued with, or attacked. Since the common responses to criticism are so destructive to communication and relationships, try these instead:

1. **Ask for details.** Criticisms are often vague or given in generalities. So if she says to you, *"You're lazy"* or *"I don't like the way you're acting,"* you can ask for details to find out exactly what she is talking about. *"Can you please tell me more?"* or *"Would you please be more specific so I can understand?"* Suggest possible complaints and ask whether these might be the problem. *"Are you upset because I didn't pay enough attention to you at the party?"* Your wife or partner says, *"You're rude."* Respond, *"Yeah, sometimes I can be rude. I know that. But what have I done just now that sounds rude to you?"*

2. **Agree with the accurate part of the criticism.** A second step to handling criticism effectively is to agree with the part of the criticism that is true. Suppose you go to a movie and you liked the movie but your girlfriend criticizes you for liking it. Instead of getting defensive, say *"Yeah, I like these adventure movies; I guess we have different taste in movies. Are you saying that you want to have more say in the kind of movies we see?"*

3. **If she is right, apologize!** This is the most mature and adult thing to do. There is no shame in acknowledging mistakes, so long as it is accompanied by a genuine effort to correct them.

GENERAL GUIDELINES FOR HANDLING CRITICISM

1. Learn to see criticism as an opportunity to learn and grow.

2. Try to avoid being defensive.

3. Listen actively.

4. Watch nonverbal language.

5. Monitor physical and emotional cues.

6. Act, do not react.

Practice "constructive and nondefensive responses" to the following four situations:

1. Your wife says to you, *"You don't help much with the housework around here."*

2. Your girlfriend has made dinner for both of you. You told her you would be home at 6:30. After you come home an hour late from playing basketball, she says, *"I don't know why I bother to treat you well. You should have been home when you told me you would be!"*

3. You are getting phone calls from an old girlfriend and not doing anything to discourage them. Your wife says, *"You obviously care a lot more about her than you do about me. You tell her to stop calling this house!"*

4. You drove home after having too many beers. Your wife says, *"That was so stupid. Don't you even care about me or the kids?"*

KEEPING TRACK

Handout

Keep a record of a situation that upset you during the week. Record the information below. This should include situation and date; body reactions (physical feeling); self-talk; how you felt about what you did; best way to handle it. As you think about it, record what you would *like* to have done in this situation.

Situation & date	
Body reactions (physical feelings)	
Self-talk	
How I felt (emotions)	
What I did	
The best way to handle it	

HOMEWORK

 **Handout**

Write down two examples of situations when you thought that your wife or girlfriend was being critical. Write down your feelings and whether the criticism was constructive or destructive. Describe exactly how you handled it: your self-talk, your feelings, and your responses. Discuss how you might have handled it better.

Criticism

Self-talk

Feelings

Your response

Better response

Criticism

Self-talk

Feelings

Your response

Better response

Session 16

EXPRESSING FEELINGS AND ACTIVE LISTENING

MATERIALS

"Weekly Check-in"
The Great Santini *video* (father/mother expressing feelings; begin at 48:23, end at 54:05)
"Expressing Your Feelings"
"Active Listening"

GOAL

To learn to express feelings and to listen to the feelings of others.

TASKS

1. *Review "Weekly Check-in."*
2. *Review homework.*
3. *Play* The Great Santini *video (father/mother expressing feelings; begin at 48:23, end at 54:05), and discuss.*
4. *Review "Expressing Your Feelings." Role-play and discuss.*
5. *Review "Active Listening."*
6. *Model and role-play active listening examples.*
7. *Assign homework.*

PROGRAM

1. Play *The Great Santini* (father/mother expressing feelings; begin at 48:23, end at 54:05), and discuss (thanks to James A. Reavis, Psy.D. for the following discussion guidelines).
   a. Discuss the Great Santini's genuine desire to emotionally connect with his son, as well as his absolute inability to do so. This is a man who is simply unable to identify or express his own emotions.

b. Compare his effort with that of his wife, who is perfectly able to tell her son how much she loves him. From her, Ben *knows* that he is loved, he develops the potential to connect with others in this way, and he develops emotional confidence and self-assurance.

c. Discuss the ways in which group members were exposed to different styles of emotional communication. Review Dutton's research (Dutton & Golant, 1995) on domestic violence offenders and their relationships with their fathers: it is filled with examples of shameful episodes and emotional distance.

d. Ask the group members what models for emotional expression they want to offer their sons.

2. Review the "Expressing Your Feelings" handout. Role-play the different situations. Review assertive and nonassertive ways of expressing feelings in these situations. Discuss the different ways we decide whether or not a situation is worth a response.

3. Review the "Active Listening" handout. Explain the basic concepts, then model and role-play active listening based on the different examples.

EXPRESSING YOUR FEELINGS

 **Handout**

For each situation below, identify your feelings.

Put into words how you might express your feelings. Remember to use "I feel" statements. Remember that you don't always have to respond. If you would choose to say nothing in any of these situations, describe your feelings instead.

1. Your girlfriend was going to meet you downtown for lunch, and you have been waiting over an hour. She finally arrives and says she had a few errands to run before she came.

2. A friend of yours makes a "joking" comment about how your wife is "a little on the hefty side."

3. Your wife teases you in front of your friends about how much trouble you have trying to fix things around the house.

4. You are late getting home and your wife or partner demands an explanation, but as soon as you begin she interrupts and starts yelling and saying how inconsiderate you are.

ACTIVE LISTENING

Handout

Active listening is a communication technique that encourages the other person to continue speaking. It also enables you to be certain you understand what the other person is saying. It's a way of checking it out. It's called *active* listening because you not only listen but also *actively* let the other person know that you have really heard her.

Active Listening Involves Paraphrasing
Paraphrasing is stating in your own words what you think the other person has said.

> *"You sound really (feeling)   about   (situation) ."*
> *"You must really feel   (feeling)   ."*
> *"What I hear you saying is _____ ."*

Active Listening Also Involves Clarifying
> *Clarifying* involves asking questions to get more information.
> *Clarifying* helps you hear more specifics about the situation and feelings.
> *Clarifying* also lets the other person know you are interested in what he or she is saying.
> *"So, tell me what happened that got you so upset."*
> *"How did you feel when that happened?"*

Active Listening Often Involves Personalizing
1. *Personalizing* involves offering a personal example of feeling the same thing or being in the same situation.

> *"I think I know what you mean. I've been there too."*
> *"I felt the same way when I lost my job. I think everyone does."*

2. *Personalizing* helps the other person feel less alone, and it implies that someone else has experienced the same thing and recovered from it.

3. *Personalizing* can be harmful if you talk *too* much about yourself and steal the spotlight from the person who needs it.

> *"You think that was bad? Listen to what happened to me!"*

Active Listening Does *Not* Mean Cheering Up, Defending Oneself, Judging the Person, or Just Repeating Back Exactly What Was Said

> All I ever do is the dirty work around here!
> *"Oh, come on, it's a hot day, you're just in a bad mood, don't worry about it."*

> You can't trust anyone around this place!
> *"Now, now, it's OK. It's all going to be better—I'll take care of it for you."*

> I'm really worried that my family is going to be mad at me for dropping out of school.
> *"You shouldn't feel that way."*

> I keep trying to talk to you about how to handle the kids and you never listen to me!
> *"I'm in charge! No more discussion!"*

> This place is really disgusting.
> *"It sounds like you think this place is really disgusting."*

Some Keys to Being a Good Active Listener
Good eye contact, slightly forward lean, reinforce by nodding or paraphrasing, clarify by asking questions, avoid distractions, try to really understand what was said.

HOMEWORK

 **Handout**

Record three examples of some "Active Listening" responses over the next week, noting in each case the situation and what you said.

1. *Situation:*

   You Said:

2. *Situation:*

   You Said:

3. *Situation:*

   You Said:

Session 17

WIVES AND PARTNERS' GROUP

MATERIALS

"Weekly Check-in"

GOAL

To help the group members gain as clear an understanding as possible of what the other person is experiencing during a fight or abusive situation.

TASKS

1. *Review homework.*
2. *Outline ground rules for this session.*
3. *Review "Weekly Check-in" (note this exception to the task order; the "Weekly Check-in" should be reviewed after members understand the rules).*
4. *Assign homework.*

PROGRAM

1. **Empathy For Victims.** Many of the men in our groups have deficits in empathy. Their behavior might be quite different if they were genuinely aware of the effect of their behavior on the other people around them. You might consider saying something like the following as an introduction to this session:

   The reason why each of you is here is because, at some point in the past, you have done something that felt hurtful to your wife or partner. We all have. At the time, you simply may not have been aware of how you were affecting your wife or partner, or what it must have been like to be in her position. We'd like to help you gain more of that knowledge, so that the next time around you'll be better informed. If you knew then what you know now (or what you are now learning), you might have made other choices.

2. The instructions are quite simple:

> *This is the "Wives and Partners'" group. We have invited you all here today to hear your side of the story. We've heard a lot about what's happened in your family from your husband's or partner's point of view. Now we'd like to hear exactly how you felt and what you went through.*

A group member describes an interpersonal conflict situation from the point of view of his partner. All the group members play the role of their own wife or partner. The entire group (or at least one hour) is conducted in this role-playing fashion.

Each group member must describe exactly what his wife or partner is thinking or feeling—without sarcasm, without editorial comments, without trying to make her look bad. The group should keep giving feedback until they think he has played the role just right and has **truly gotten inside the other person's shoes**.

The goal here is not problem solving, but rather understanding. It is also important to remind the men that gaining an empathic point of view does not necessarily mean agreeing with the other person, but simply understanding what it must feel like to *be* that person.

3. One way to structure this exercise is to make notes on the board when you review the "Weekly check-in" at the beginning of the group. These notes describe the wife's or partner's point of view in the argument. Then use these for the empathy training exercise. For example:

- Carrie is suspicious because another woman has been calling me.
- Denise gets on my case about going off to play basketball.
- Nina insisted on watching her TV show even though she knew it was time for ESPN SportsCenter.

4. Encourage all the group members to join in with questions and discussion of their fellow "wives and partners."

HOMEWORK

Handout

Write one paragraph (at least 100 words) as if you are your wife or girlfriend. The subject is "Sometimes I don't trust my husband (or partner) because . . ."

Session 18
THE FOUR HORSEMEN OF THE APOCALYPSE

MATERIALS

"Weekly Check-in"
"The Four Horsemen of the Apocalypse"
"Keeping a Positive Perspective on Your Partner"
"Repair Attempts Questionnaire"

GOAL

To teach the men about destructive patterns in marital communication; to help them identify these patterns and recognize the negative self-talk that accompanies them.

TASKS

1. *Review "Weekly Check-in."*
2. *Review homework.*
3. *Read and review "The Four Horsemen of the Apocalypse."*
4. *Read and review "Keeping a Positive Perspective on Your Partner."*
5. *Read and review "Repair Attempts Questionnaire."*
6. *Assign homework.*

PROGRAM

Research by Dr. John Gottman and his colleagues (Gottman, 1994; Gottman, Coan et al, 1998; Gottman, Jacobson et al, 1995) has helped us understand patterns in marital communication which are almost sure to doom a marriage. The "Four Horsemen of the Apocalypse" handout explains the basic principles and examples of these communication patterns. Use the handout as a discussion guide for understanding how this works. Ask the men to identify themselves and their partners in these examples.

Make sure to (1) identify the self-talk patterns that govern these patterns, and (2) role-play alternatives for how to use different self-talk and different communications.

Clearly highlight the following two main points:

1. Review the communication patterns of the "Four Horsemen of the Apocalypse." Emphasize that the men should be able to identify these patterns and try and reduce them in their relationships.

2. Discuss the "secret, silent decision" (see "Keeping a Positive Perspective on Your Partner"). Discuss how the narratives that people have in relationships determine their emotional and behavioral reactions.

THE FOUR HORSEMEN OF THE APOCALYPSE*

 **Handout**

ACCUSATIONS (CRITICISM)

Accusations are expressed in a destructive manner, as an attack on the other person's character: *"You're so thoughtless and self-centered!"*

In an accusation, you state specifically what is upsetting you and criticize the other person's action, not the person herself, saying how it made you feel.

CONTEMPT (DISGUST)

Contempt is usually expressed not just in words themselves, but also in a tone of voice and an angry expression: rolling the eyes, a look of disgust.

What distinguishes *contempt* is the *intention to insult* and *psychologically abuse* the other person. When contempt begins to overwhelm the relationship, you tend to forget entirely the other person's positive qualities, at least when feeling upset. You can't remember a single positive quality or act.

DEFENSIVENESS

Defensiveness is the fighting back response. Here you refuse to take in anything the other person is saying. It is one arm of the typical "fight-or-flight" response.

Defensiveness feels like an understandable reaction to feeling besieged—this is why it is so destructive. The "victim" doesn't see anything wrong with being defensive, even though this attitude escalates a conflict rather than leads to resolution. Defensive people never say, "*Maybe you're right,*" or "*I see your point,*" or "*Yeah, I get it. I think I owe you an apology.*"

STONEWALLING

Stonewalling is the ultimate defense. The stonewaller just goes blank and withdraws from the conversation. This sends a powerful message: icy distance, superiority, and distaste. Don't confuse stonewalling with time-out. Time-out communicates *respect*. The message is that you care enough about the relationship to make special efforts not to cause any further damage. And there is a very clear contract that the discussion *will* continue at a future time.

HOW SUCCESSFUL RELATIONSHIPS WORK

Research indicates that successful relationships manage to express appreciation, soften complaints, respond nondefensively, back down, and use humor.

---

*Based on ideas from Gottman (2000).

KEEPING A POSITIVE PERSPECTIVE ON YOUR PARTNER

 Handout

In dysfunctional couples, negative mind reading runs rampant. It is as if each partner has made a "secret, silent decision" about the other that he or she is an adversary and not worth respecting. They each assume the worst about the other.

Let's say that you ask your wife to stop at the store to get some things on her way home. She responds with an attitude, as though this is a big burden on her.

An ally's self-talk goes something like this: *"Oh well, she is in a bad mood. She has been under a lot of stress lately and needs more sleep."* Her negativity is viewed as unstable (highly alterable, fluctuating), and the cause is viewed as situational (external).

On the other hand, in an unhappy marriage, the same behavior is likely to be interpreted as stable (enduring, unchanging) and internal to her. The accompanying thought might be something like this, *"She is inconsiderate and selfish. That's the way she is. That's why she did that."*

Each of these factors adds to the strength of the relationship alliance:

- High frequency of spontaneous expressions of fondness and admiration
- Low frequency of spontaneous expressions of disappointment and negativity
- High degree of "we-ness" in the couple's conversations
- Low levels of couples describing their lives as chaotic and out of control
- Low degree of differences related to gender issues (*"Women shouldn't act that way"*, *"I expect the man in my life to be like this"*, *"Why aren't you more of a man/woman?"*)
- A good-sized "emotional bank account": how much credit each person has built up by positive relationship behaviors

---

*Based on ideas from Gottman (2000).

REPAIR ATTEMPTS QUESTIONNAIRE*

Handout

To assess the effectiveness of your repair attempts in your own relationship, answer the following questions using the seven-point scale at the bottom of the page.

1. We are good at taking breaks when we need them.

2. My partner usually accepts my apologies.

3. I can say that I am wrong.

4. I am pretty good at calming myself down.

5. We can maintain a sense of humor.

6. When my partner says we should talk to each other differently, it usually makes sense.

7. My attempts to repair our discussions when they get negative are usually effective.

8. We are pretty good listeners even when we have different positions on things.

9. If things get heated, we can usually pull out of it and change things.

10. My spouse is good at soothing me when I get upset.

11. I feel confident that we can resolve most issues between us.

12. When I comment on how we could communicate better my spouse listens to me.

13. Even if things get hard at times I know we can get past our differences.

14. We can be affectionate even when we are disagreeing.

15. Teasing and humor usually work to get my spouse over negativity.

16. We can start all over again and improve our discussion when we need to.

17. When emotions run hot, expressing how upset I feel makes a real difference.

18. We can discuss even big differences between us.

19. My partner expresses appreciation for nice things I do.

20. If I keep trying to communicate it will eventually work.

Never			Sometimes			Definitely
1	2	3	4	5	6	7

6 "true" answers or above: This is an area of strength in your marriage. When marital discussions are at a risk of getting out of hand, you are able to put on the brakes and effectively calm each other down.

Below 6 "true" answers: Your marriage could stand some improvement in this area. By learning how to repair your interactions when negativity engulfs you, you can dramatically improve the effectiveness of your problem solving and develop a more positive perspective of each other and your marriage.

---

*From Gottman (2000), pp. 170–72.

HOMEWORK

Handout

Fill out the "Repair Attempts Questionnaire" and be prepared to discuss it in the next session.

Session 19
THE RIGHT TRACK/CONTEXT OF COMPETENCE

MATERIALS

"Weekly Check-in"
"Keeping the Train on the Right Track"
"The Context of Competence"

GOAL

To teach the men creative ways to repair their relationships and identify the strengths in their partners, their relationships, and themselves.

TASKS

1. *Review "Weekly Check-in."*
2. *Review homework.*
3. *Read and review "Keeping the Train on the Right Track."*
4. *Read and review "The Context of Competence."*
5. *Assign homework.*

PROGRAM

1. Review "Keeping the Train on the Right Track." Discuss examples of "repair mechanisms." Point out that all couples have unique ways in which they soothe or soften conversations that otherwise might blow up. Some of these are specific verbal statements, and others are behaviors such as physical affection, distraction, ganging up on somebody else, self-deprecating humor, engaging in joint tasks, giving space, and not getting in the last word. As an exercise, ask the men to generate personal examples of how this works in their own relationships.

2. Review and discuss "The Context of Competence." Ask group members to apply these principles to situations in their own lives. Go around the room and discuss examples. It is usually helpful to bring in current examples that have already been discussed in this session or in recent sessions.

KEEPING THE TRAIN ON THE RIGHT TRACK*

 **Handout**

Through their words, body language, tone of voice, and subtle behaviors, people can communicate a fundamental message of acceptance: *"Please don't worry—I really like you and I really love you."* Once that basic message is established, they can afford to move on to the issue at hand: *"I don't like this specific behavior and I'd like you to change it."* For the most part, the partner can handle this because it is not perceived as a fundamental threat. The fundamental sense of appreciation serves as an antithreat device.

"I STILL LOVE YOU" GESTURES

> Joining together
> Physical affection
> The cup of coffee
> Self-deprecating humor

CHANGING THE SUBJECT

> Turning attention to somebody else
> Allowing space
> Distraction

NOT MAKING A BAD MOMENT EVEN WORSE

> Staying in the present
> Forfeiting the last word
> Ignoring the negative

Successful couples have a remarkable capacity for generating soothing, nonthreatening responses that keep the relationship on the right track. It never fails to surprise and delight me to hear some new way that a couple stays connected that I would never have dreamed of. The best techniques are invented by real couples, not self-help authors.

Good relationship strategies apply just as much to men as they do to women. There are hundreds of books and articles that teach sound principles for positive communication. Following are 10 of my favorite strategies, simply based on what successful couples seem to do that works. In addition to applying some of these strategies, try looking at what you and your partner already do that works.

"I STILL LOVE YOU" GESTURES

Joining Together

Marie was feeling frustrated and irritated that the house was messy and the hall closet was totally disorganized. Cory had said he would clean the closet. She started to snap at him; he got defensive. Then she stopped herself. She softened. She said to him, *"I have an idea. Let's start working on this together. I'll go through these things, you tell me what you think we can throw out."* And it worked, because they became engaged in the project together. And Marie resisted the temptation to turn this into an *I'm-getting-screwed* narrative; instead, it became a *we're-in-this-together* story.

Physical Affection

Darren and his girlfriend, Michelle, were arguing about how he had treated her in front of her family. Darren was acting very defensive because he felt stupid and exposed. Although he did not say so, he felt worried that Michelle had really lost respect for him, and this was unbearable to him. Michelle sensed this. She reached over and stroked his arm, and his defensiveness melted. Her touch communicated that of course she still loved him, which allowed him to let his guard down and really listen to what she had to say.

I have heard some couples describe a similar sequence at the end of an evening of arguing. They go to bed with icy feelings in the room, backs turned to each other (despite what their mothers told them about never going to bed angry). Then one of them takes a chance, turns around, and snuggles up in the spoon position. No passionate sex required. The tension dissolves as the receiving partner gets the message: "*It's okay, I still love you, we're going to be all right.*"

The Cup of Coffee

This is a variation on the physical affection approach. You have an argument. The room feels tense. You are not looking at each other or talking to each other. You go into the kitchen and come back with a cup of coffee for your wife—or a glass of water, piece of pizza, or the magazine she left downstairs. This is an olive branch, again with the unspoken message of "*It's okay, I still love you, we're going to be all right.*"

Self-deprecating Humor

Johnny and his wife, Takeesha, were driving with their kids to a family gathering at a place they had never been before. It was really important to Takeesha that they not be late, and she had told Johnny this several times. He was driving and she was trying to give him directions, but they were getting more and more lost. She wanted to stop for directions, but he thought he could figure it out himself, and they became later and later. They started snapping at each other. He blamed her for not giving him the right directions; she blamed him for not listening to what she told him and for being a bullheaded guy who refused to ask for help.

When they finally arrived at the party, late and apologetic, the kids were fighting and the tension between Johnny and Takeesha was thick. When someone asked them what happened, they glared at each other. Then Johnny got a sheepish grin on his face and stepped up to the plate. "It was just me having too much testosterone and not asking for directions. Next time I'll listen to my wife." Takeesha looked at him, and then they both laughed, and the day was rescued.

CHANGING THE SUBJECT

Turning Attention to Somebody Else

Michelle came home from work and complained about how much of a mess the house was. She was on a rampage, going off on both Darren and the kids for not cleaning up enough. Then she told Darren, "*I can't believe I have to come home to this on top of getting hassled all day by my supervisor!*" Darren seized the opportunity and said, "*What color were her fingernails today? Are they still that purple color that goes with her hair?*" Michelle laughed. They were launched on a trash-the-supervisor session, which helped break the mood and join them together. This is one situation in which gossip and cattiness come in very handy.

My kids like to pull this one on me. Both of them are in bad moods, and they start hassling each other. I have one goal and one goal only: for all military action to yield to an immediate cease-fire. So I launch into some psychobabble, trying to find out what started it all and reminding them that all it takes is for one of them to not react and this whole thing will die down. And then they turn on me!

> She: "*Dad always has the lamest little words of wisdom! I can't believe he thinks that's going to work on us!*"
> He: "*Can you believe any of his clients ever put up with that? It's so stupid!*"

The subject has changed. They join forces. I pretend to be miffed, but I am secretly grinning. I have thrown myself on the grenade and the battle has ended. Pretty soon they will forgive me for my "ineptitude" and we will be back to some sort of equilibrium.

Allowing Space

Just backing off and giving some space when your wife or girlfriend is upset and haranguing you can sometimes be the most effective strategy. Many couples have mastered the art of stepping aside and waiting for the storm to pass. This does not qualify as a problem-solving technique, nor does it qualify as a path toward exploring the deeper feelings and issues that triggered the conflict in the first place. But many successful couples do it, and you can't argue with success.

Younger couples often balk at this strategy, objecting that this is just sweeping things under the rug. Couples who have been around for a while smile in recognition. They know that successful relationships value "selective blindness" to irritations as much as they address the occasional important issues that cannot be ignored.

Distraction

The same could be said for distraction. Perhaps you have learned how to steer the subject away from the difficult topic; again, many successful couples do this all the time. They pick their battles, because when tempers are starting to flare, there is usually very little to be gained and much at risk.

NOT MAKING A BAD MOMENT EVEN WORSE

Staying in the Present

Another essential strategy used by many successful couples is keeping the argument specific and in the present: *"It really bothered me that you didn't call this afternoon to tell me you were going to be late"* rather than *"You never think about anyone but yourself."*

Forfeiting the Last Word

Successful couples also have a remarkable capacity for not insisting on getting the last word. When both of you insist on the last word, the last words go onto infinity. When one person manages to let the last-word opportunity go by, the game is usually over. Just leaving well enough alone is a key strategy in successful relationship damage control and is evidence of emotional intelligence.

Ignoring the Negative

Think of the men who called home to say hello to his wife. He began the conversation by simply saying *"Hi!"* Her response, bitter and tense, was *"Don't you 'Hi!' me!"* Her tone was not the least bit humorous.

What were his options for reacting to this?

1. Tell himself that this is one more example of how emotionally unstable his wife is—and emotionally withdraw from her.

2. Tell himself that he doesn't need this crap, that she doesn't understand anything about what his needs are, that he was just trying to be friendly, and complain that she should be a hell of a lot nicer to him.

3. Take a deep breath and remember that this is not typical for her and that she must be having a very bad day, then ask her what's wrong, as if she has said, *"I'm in a terrible mood—just leave me alone!"*

The correct answer is 3. When your partner's behavior is completely over-the-top, your best bet is to just let it go by and instead react compassionately to the feelings underneath the behavior.

---

*Adapted from Wexler (2004), pp. 174–81.

THE CONTEXT OF COMPETENCE

Handout

The philosophy of the "context of competence" is to catch yourself doing something right. Even when you and your partner have made mistakes or behaved destructively in your relationship, it is very valuable to still identify the parts that went right—and build on these strengths.

> *"Even though I yelled at my wife, I was able to stop myself from threatening her or becoming physical. How was I successful at stopping myself here?"*
>
> *"Even though we had a big blowout, we were able to end it pretty quickly—and after about an hour we were pretty much over it. How were we successful at recovering so quickly?"*

In analyzing a relationship problem, it is also very helpful to identify the strengths that already exist.

> **Past success:** *"What have we done in the past that was successful?"*
>
> **Positive exceptions:** *"Even though we argue a lot about money, when are we able to talk about money without arguing?"*
>
> **Coping statements:** *"What do we already know about how to handle these issues successfully?"*
>
> **Scaling questions:** *"I know we still bicker and criticize each other, but it's happening less frequently (or doesn't last as long, or never gets as bad as it used to)."*

HOMEWORK

 **Handout**

Identify three situations when you used one of the "repair mechanisms" in communicating with your wife or partner or someone else. Describe the situation and what you said and did.

1.   **Situation**

   You said (or did)

2.   **Situation**

   You said (or did)

3.   **Situation**

   You said (or did)

Session 20

COMPLIMENTS: GIVING AND RECEIVING

MATERIALS

"Weekly Check-in"
"Dealing with Compliments"

GOALS

To teach the men the value of giving and receiving compliments; to help them identify ways in which they deflect the value of compliments, and ways in which they could offer compliments more effectively.

TASKS

1. Review "Weekly Check-in."

2. Review homework.

3. Explain types of compliments.

4. Review handout "Dealing with Compliments."

5. Model deflections of compliments.

6. Encourage discussion of self-talk attitudes about compliments.

7. Lead exercise in offering compliments.

8. Assign homework.

PROGRAM

1. Explain how assertiveness includes the ability to offer clear and direct compliments to other people—and to find ways to truly accept the compliments of others. Define compliments: generate specific examples of different kinds of compliments, including those on appearance, behavior, and basic personality.

2. Review "Dealing with Compliments." Explain the "assertive" way of dealing with compliments: accept and reward. As an exercise, ask the men to offer you a compliment—and then model an example of one defensive response. To make it more

entertaining, ask for a different compliment from each group member until you have modeled all five defensive responses. Ask the group members to discuss personal examples of these responses.

3. Now review the self-talk that makes it difficult for people to give compliments, such as, "I never got very much praise, why should I give it?" or to receive them, such as, "People will think I'm full of myself."

4. Make sure to discuss the ways in which compliments can be used in a manipulative fashion, and why some people are so mistrusting of compliments. Role-play examples of group members using compliments genuinely and manipulatively in their marriages.

5. Go around the room and ask each group member to offer a genuine compliment to the three group members on his right. Direct the group's attention to the ways in which compliments are both offered and received.

DEALING WITH COMPLIMENTS

Handout

ASSERTIVE RESPONSES

Accepting compliments is one sign of assertiveness, which can help us feel better about ourselves. The purpose of this exercise is to examine what happens to us when we are given a sincere compliment and when we give one to another person.

   Accept and Reward: This is the most assertive and positive response to compliments. It usually means saying *"Thanks. I appreciate that"* and looking pleased. The key to this style is that you feel good and you make the *other* person feel good for complimenting you. He or she will want to do it again.

DEFENSIVE RESPONSES

   Refuse: *"Oh, that old thing?"* or *"I'm really messing up—I just cover it up well."* This kind of refusal gives the message that the person offering the compliment is wrong or that his perceptions are off. Is the other person likely to compliment you again?

   Deflect: This involves body language: tossing the compliment away by looking down with the eyes or shrugging the shoulders. Another way is to just ignore the compliment completely and show no signs of taking it in.

   Automatic return: This is a common way that people deal with the discomfort of receiving the compliment. Here, you blurt out *"Oh, thanks, you look nice, too!"* so fast that it seems phony and forced. There is nothing wrong with offering someone else a compliment in return, but saying it too quickly or searching too hard doesn't work.

   Becoming suspicious: You know that sometimes people will try to manipulate you with compliments. If this has been done to you in the past, you may become automatically suspicious even when there is no reason to be. You may always wonder, "What does she want from me now?"

   Big shot: Because the compliment makes you nervous, you cover up those feelings and say, *"Damn straight! I* am *the strongest dude in town! And you know—women* are *crazy about me! So you've got good taste!"* Who would ever want to give this guy a compliment again?

HOMEWORK

 **Handout**

Record three compliments you receive over the next week. Describe your self-talk and your response to each compliment.

1. Compliment:

   Self-talk:

   Response:

2. Compliment:

   Self-talk:

   Response:

3. Compliment:

   Self-talk:

   Response:

Session 21
CONFLICT WITH RESPECT

MATERIALS

"Weekly Check-in"
Rules for the "Softened Start-up Statement"
"Conflict with Respect"
"Who Decides?"

GOALS

To introduce a cognitive structure for couple communication and problem solving; to create a nonthreatening atmosphere in which men can reveal their specific relationship and communication difficulties.

TASKS

1. *Review "Weekly Check-in."*
2. *Review homework.*
3. *Review the "Softened Start-up" rules and role-play.*
4. *Review "Conflict with Respect."*
5. *Model and role-play examples of "dealing straight," including the "wrong" way to do it.*
6. *Review "Who Decides?"*
7. *Assign homework.*

PROGRAM

1. Review the "Softened Start-up" rules and role-play.

2. Review "Conflict with Respect" model and role-play examples of each, including the "wrong" way of doing it. Use this session to review many of the communication principles the group has already learned.

3. Review the "Who Decides?" questionnaire and responses in group discussion.

RULES FOR THE "SOFTENED START-UP" STATEMENT*

Handout

- Be concise.
- In the initial start-up complaint sentence, complain but don't blame.
- Start with something positive.
- Make statements that start with "I" instead of "you."
- Describe what is happening, don't evaluate or judge.
- Talk clearly about what you need.
- Be polite.
- Express appreciation.
- Don't store things up.
- Restate your feelings in terms of the more vulnerable emotions.

---

*Based on ideas from Gottman (2000), pp. 164–66.

CONFLICT WITH RESPECT

 Handout

Arguments can be a useful way to solve problems, or they can be never-ending battles that can increase tension and the risk of abuse. The central theme here, as always, is *respect*. Can you offer your partner respect even when you're upset? The following guidelines can make a difference:

USE FAIR BEHAVIOR (RESPECT)

- Let your partner know what you want to discuss.
- All subjects are OK. Make "I" statements, owning your thoughts and feelings.
- Speak one at a time and allow equal time.
- Use "active listening": reflect back what your partner is probably thinking and feeling.
- Look for compromises.
- Talk about the here-and-now.
- Refer only to the immediate problem—don't bring in the past.
- Make room for time-outs and breaks.
- Give your reasons and offer solutions.
- Admit when you're wrong.
- When you have come to an agreement, repeat it or write it down to make sure both of you are clear about it.
- Finish the argument, even if it means taking a time-out along the way.

HOW TO AVOID UNFAIR BEHAVIOR (DISRESPECT)

- Do not use name-calling or put-downs.
- Do not drag up old wounds from the past.
- Stay on track; do not go off in different directions.
- Do not threaten or intimidate.
- Do not assume that you will either win or lose this argument.
- Do not save up all your gripes to dump on your partner all at once.
- Be careful of "mind-reading" self-talk. Don't *assume* the most negative things about your partner. *Ask!*
- Do not deny the facts. Come clean.
- Do not gloat over a "victory" in getting your way.
- Do not sulk, ignore, pout, withdraw, or give your partner the silent treatment.

WHO DECIDES?*

Handout

Check below whether you think an item should be your decision, your partner's decision, or open to negotiation. Remember that there are no right or wrong answers here, so long as both partners agree about the decision-making process.

	Your decision	Mostly yours	Joint decision	Mostly hers	Your partner's decision
1. Which friends can she spend time with?					
2. Which friends can you spend time with?					
3. Can she drink on certain occasions?					
4. Can you drink on certain occasions?					
5. Who decides on a sitter for the children?					
6. Will she get a job/go to school?					
7. Will you get a job/go to school?					

*Adapted with permission from Pence & Paymar (1993), p. 160.

	Your decision	Mostly yours	Joint decision	Mostly hers	Your partner's decision
8. How will she dress when she leaves the house?					
9. How will you dress when you leave the house?					
10. How will the children be disciplined?					
11. What is your paycheck spent on?					
12. What is her paycheck spent on?					

HOMEWORK

 Handout

Practice a "softened start-up" approach three times. Record both the statements and your partner's response.

1. My "softened start-up" statement:

Response from my partner:

2. My "softened start-up" statement:

Response from my partner:

3. My "softened start-up" statement:

Response from my partner:

Session 22

HURTING THE ONES YOU LOVE

MATERIALS

"Weekly Check-in"
Emotional Abuse and Mind Games
Relationship Respect Contract

GOAL

To help the group members recognize how and why they may do emotional damage to the people they love the most.

TASKS

---

1. *Review "Weekly Check-in."*
2. *Review homework.*
3. *Review and discuss "Emotional Abuse & Mind-Games."*
4. *Conduct "Hurting the Ones You Love" exercise.*
5. *Discuss "Relationship Respect Contract."*
6. *Assign homework.*

PROGRAM

1. Review and discuss "Emotional Abuse & Mind-Games."

2. Guide the group members through the following exercise (adapted from Stosny, personal communication, 2001):

   Recall the most hurtful thing you have ever done or said to a loved one. All of us have certainly said or done something hurtful to a parent, child, wife, or girlfriend. Close your eyes for a moment and recall that event. . . . Now imagine strangers doing or saying that same thing to that person. How would you respond?

The typical response among many group members is, "I'd kill them." Attachment includes an automatic instinct to protect, which is why, without thinking about it, we would jump in front of a bullet to protect our children.

Then ask:

Isn't it confusing to realize that some of the very mean things you have done—to the people you love the most—are the ones that you would be most outraged by if you observed someone else doing them?

Use this basic exercise as a springboard for a discussion about the extremely confusing and conflicted pattern of hurting people whom you love.

Also ask the group members to identify the specific scene they visualized, and to identify specifically how they might have reacted if they observed someone else acting this way to their partner or kids. This is an excellent opportunity to hear how clearly the group members can identify their own past abusive behavior.

3. Review and discuss "Relationship Respect Contract."

EMOTIONAL ABUSE AND MIND GAMES

Handout

As with physical abuse, repeated emotional abuse can have severe effects on the victim's sense of self and sense of reality. These mind games sometimes leave more lasting damage than physical abuse. The person on the receiving end, male or female, may question his or her reality, feel powerless, and become overdependent. Here are some examples:

COERCION

- *"I am going to kill myself if you leave me!"*
- *"Either you put out for me or I'm going to go find someone who will!"*
- *"I'm gonna take these kids right now and you'll never see them again!"*
- *"I'll get a doctor to say you're crazy and put you away!"*

PUT-DOWNS

- *"You're just like your mother: a fat, brainless ass!"*
- *"You're just like your father: a lazy, bull-headed ass!"*
- *"My wife can't cook for shit." (in front of other people)*
- *"My mother was right about you—you'll never amount to anything!"*
- *"How come a big, strong guy like you can't make more money around here?"*
- *"You're acting crazy."*
- *"There you go again—crying like a big baby."*
- *"Nobody's ever going to want you!"*

ISOLATION

- *"I want to know everywhere you've been in the last 24 hours!"*
- *"I want to know where every penny has been spent!"*
- *"I know you go to that school just so you can try to pick up some girl!"*
- *"Your family just messes you up—I don't ever want you to talk to them again!"*
- *"No, you can't have the car. I might need it and you don't need to go anywhere."*
- *"You can't go out. I want you to stay right at home with me."*

BLAMING

- *"It's your fault my career is going nowhere."*
- *"Nobody else has ever made me violent! You must be doing something to cause this!"*

MALE PRIVILEGE AND CONTROL

- *"You don't even know how to take care of yourself without me around!"*
- *"You have not cleaned up this house properly!"*
- *"No wife of mine is going out to work—that's my job!"*
- *"I don't care what you think about my gambling—it's my money and I'll do what I want!"*
- *"So what if I bought that car without discussing it with you?"*

RELATIONSHIP RESPECT CONTRACT

 **Handout**

We agree to help build our relationship, and we recognize that this will not be successful if any of the following behaviors take place:

1. Any incidents of direct physical abuse or violence.

2. Any direct or implied threats of physical abuse or violence (to self, other, or property).

3. Any direct or implied threats to behave in a way that would be extremely harmful to the other person (such as exposing personal secrets).

4. Any physical restrictions on either party's freedom of movement.

5. Any significant property destruction as an expression of aggression.

6. Any threats to leave the relationship (except for temporary time-outs to defuse a tense situation).

7. Any pattern of extreme verbal put-downs or humiliation of the other person.

8. Any acts of infidelity or actions which suggest the possibility of infidelity.

9. Other _____

Both parties also agree to make all reasonable efforts to focus on building the positive aspects of the relationship.

_____   _____
                                             Date

_____   _____
                                             Date

_____   _____
Witness (optional)   Date

HOMEWORK

Review the "Relationship Respect Contract" with your partner. Discus each item to make sure that both understand and agree. If there is any item that you do not agree on, cross it off. If there are additional ones you both want, add them to the list. Sign the contract. If you are not currently in a relationship, edit the contract in the way that you would like it to be for your next relationship.

Session 23
APOLOGIES

MATERIALS

"Weekly Check-in"
"The Art of Apologies"
"Classic Apology Mistakes"

GOAL

To help group members develop effective and mature ways of offering apologies in an intimate relationship.

TASKS

1. *Review "Weekly Check-in."*
2. *Review homework.*
3. *Explain principles of effective apologies.*
4. *Review "The Art of Apologies."*
5. *Review "Classic Apology Mistakes."*
6. *Assign homework.*

PROGRAM

1. Discuss the importance of genuine apologies in close relationships. It is especially important to frame the act of apologizing as something a "real man" is secure enough and honorable enough to do.

2. Review "The Art of Apologies." Discuss each item thoroughly and review the possible exceptions to these principles.

3. Review "Classic Apology Mistakes."

4. Assign homework.

THE ART OF APOLOGIES

 **Handout**

Apologies grease the wheels of most successful relationships. The art of delivering a sincere and well-timed apology is one that all of us should be very skilled at.

The obvious trigger situation for an apology is when you realize that you have done something that has hurt someone you care about. Even if your action was not intended to hurt or you were not aware of how it would affect the other person, an apology is still in order.

An effective apology requires three distinct elements to make it more likely to be well received (which is, after all, the point of the apology in the first place):

THE BASIC STATEMENT

"I'm sorry." No rationalizations, no excuses, no hedging. Just a simple statement that you are sorry and what you are sorry for having done. It could be big or very minor, it doesn't matter.

Start by describing exactly what you did wrong, then just acknowledge that this was a mistake. Accept responsibility:

- *"I'm really sorry I started teasing you in front of your friends."*
- *"I feel terrible for having that affair and I am really, really sorry for how I have hurt you."*
- *"Sorry I forgot to take out the trash."*

DEMONSTRATION OF INSIGHT

You need to offer the other person some evidence that you have learned something or that there was some temporary circumstance that will not happen again, or at least that you will really be on guard against it the next time around:

- *"I think I was just feeling insecure, and this was some sort of way to make jokes and fit in. I won't let that happen again."*
- *"There's no excuse—it had everything to do with me and feeling like I'm not getting enough attention. I wish there was some way I could go back in time and talk to you about what I've been going through instead of doing what I did."*
- *"I was just really rushing around last night and I didn't pay attention. I'm going to start writing it in my appointment book to make sure I remember each week."*

BEHAVIOR CHANGE

The proof is in the pudding. All the words and all the good intentions in the world don't mean a thing unless the other person sees, over time, that you have genuinely learned something from your mistake and that you are handling the situation differently in the future: maybe not 100% perfectly, but definitely better. Remember that your partner cannot possibly feel secure until she has observed, over time, that you have changed. Obviously, the length of time that this takes is directly related to how serious the "crime" was.

CLASSIC APOLOGY MISTAKES

 Handout

1. **Not being genuine.** How do you like it when you hear "I'm sorry you feel that way" or "I'm sorry if that hurt your feelings"? Sometimes that might be OK, but most of the time this does not show sincere regret. In fact, it often makes the other person feel stupid for "overreacting" or being "too sensitive." This usually does not get a passing grade as a genuine *apology*.

2. **Crummy body language.** Maybe the words are right, but there is no eye contact or even a hostile look. Or the tone of voice sounds sarcastic. This also fails the grade.

3. **Waiting for the perfect moment.** Some people wait for the "perfect moment" for an apology. This does not exist (although it's probably best not to do it in heavy traffic or when the baby is screaming). The perfect moment to apologize is the moment you realize you've done something wrong, or as soon as possible thereafter.

4. **Expecting immediate and total forgiveness.** Remember Commandment 3: "We cannot control another person, but we can control ourselves." All you can do is give it your best and most sincere shot. She may never be able to forgive you, or it may take her a little while.

5. **Apologizing too much.** Some people apologize way too much, for the smallest things, or even when they haven't really done anything wrong. This is just plain irritating, and it's like crying wolf. The real and significant apologies will be weakened if they distract attention from real issues. This weakens meaningful apologies when the time for them arrives.

HOMEWORK

 **Handout**

Identify three apologies to offer to your wife, girlfriend, or children. Make the apology, and record the response from the other person. If you are not in contact with any of them, identify three apologies you would make if you had the opportunity.

1. Apology from you:

Response from wife, girlfriend, or child:

2. Apology from you:

Response from wife, girlfriend, or child:

3. Apology from you:

Response from wife, girlfriend, or child:

Session 24
WHAT'S UP WITH SEX?

MATERIALS

Weekly Check-in
"Sexual Abuse: Psychological and Physical"
"Masculinity Traps: Sex"
"Sexual Meaning Questionnaire"

GOAL

To help group members understand ways in which sexual expectations and demands can be destructive in an intimate relationship.

TASKS

1. *Review "Weekly Check-in."*
2. *Review homework.*
3. *Introduce definition of sexual abuse and sexual assault.*
4. *Review "Sexual Abuse: Psychological and Physical."*
5. *Review "Masculinity Traps: Sex."*
6. *Assign homework.*

PROGRAM

1. This session is particularly complicated for group discussion. Many of the group members, who may have become less defensive about general actions of psychological and physical abuse, may continue to maintain considerable defensiveness about examples of what we are describing as sexual abuse.

   Some of this is simply from ignorance or lack of awareness about why certain behaviors qualify as abusive. First of all, it is important to simply define sexual abuse: **any unwanted touching or other sexual behavior is a form of abuse.** If it involves intercourse, it is rape. If it involves physical force, it is sexual assault. It doesn't matter if the assaulter is drunk, stoned, or feeling pressured by his friends—it is still rape or sexual assault. And it doesn't matter if the two parties know each other, have had sex before, or even if they are married. It is still considered rape or sexual assault.

2. With these definitions in mind, review the "Sexual Abuse: Psychological and Physical" handout. Discuss the variety of ways in which sexual behaviors can represent an abuse of power in the relationship. Obviously, not all of the examples on the list are criminal offenses—but they represent a continuum of sexually abusive behaviors.

3. As you guide this discussion, be especially sensitive to the embarrassment or discomfort that the group members are likely to experience. Some may joke around or join in laughter with degrading comments toward women. Although it is important to set a different tone in this group, be careful about confronting too intensely—unless all else fails. Power struggles will doom this group discussion. Set an example by maintaining a serious tone yourself. Calmly remind the men of the importance of talking about these issues in ways that do not degrade or generalize. If they are able to describe examples of some of these destructive sexual behaviors in "others," this may be an acceptable way to generate valuable discussion and reflection.

4. Review "Masculinity Traps: Sex" and the "Sexual Meaning Questionnaire." It is especially important to focus on issues of entitlement and perceived peer pressure in this discussion. Refer back to Session 8 on jealousy and misinterpretations; remind the men, through examples, how crucial their self-talk is when they encounter some form of sexual frustration.

SEXUAL ABUSE: PSYCHOLOGICAL AND PHYSICAL

 Handout

Sexual abuse is one of the rooms in the "House of Abuse" that is especially difficult to talk about. Sometimes it is even difficult to know that it is taking place. Below is a sample of different forms of abusive sexual behaviors, both psychological and physical. If you can, try to be honest with yourself about which of these you may have used at some point in your relationships.

PUT-DOWNS

- Making jokes about women in your partner's presence
- Checking out other women in her presence
- Making sexual put-down jokes
- Comparing her body to those of other women or to pictures in magazines
- Criticizing sexual performance
- Blaming her if you don't feel satisfied with sex
- Using sexual labels: calling her a "slut" or "frigid"

MIND GAMES

- Telling her that agreeing to sex is the only way she can prove she has been faithful or that she still loves you
- Revealing intimate details about her to others
- Withholding sex and affection only to gain control over the other person
- Engaging in sexual affairs

PRESSURE

- Always wanting sex
- Expecting sex whenever you want it
- Demanding sex with threats
- Talking her into stripping or talking sexually in a way that feels humiliating to her
- Talking her into watching sex or pornography when this is offensive to her
- Talking her into touching others when this is offensive to her

FORCE

- Forcing touch
- Forcing sex while she's sleeping
- Touching her in ways that are uncomfortable to her
- Forcing uncomfortable sex
- Forcing sex after physical abuse
- Sex for the purpose of hurting (use of objects/weapons)

MASCULINITY TRAPS: SEX

 **Handout**

Masculinity traps	The big picture
■ *"I deserve to have sex upon demand."*	■ *"Sex involves the needs of two people, not just one."*
■ *"If my wife or girlfriend doesn't put out, it means she's trying to hurt me."*	■ *"There are many reasons why my partner may not be in the mood for sex."*
■ *"Real men get laid all the time."*	■ *"Many men talk big—real men respect the individuality of the woman they love.*
■ *"I've had a hard day. I deserve some rewards."*	■ *"I can't expect my wife to always be available exactly when I need her."*

SEXUAL MEANING QUESTIONNAIRE

 **Handout**

Rate the importance of the various functions of sex in your life by circling the number that best describes how you feel about each item.

Function of sex in your life	Not important					Very important	
1. Produce children	1	2	3	4	5	6	7
2. Orgasm for me	1	2	3	4	5	6	7
3. Orgasm for my partner	1	2	3	4	5	6	7
4. Reassurance of my masculinity	1	2	3	4	5	6	7
5. Reassure my partner of her femininity	1	2	3	4	5	6	7
6. Expression of love/warmth by me	1	2	3	4	5	6	7
7. Expression of love/warmth by her	1	2	3	4	5	6	7
8. Way to release tension	1	2	3	4	5	6	7
9. Way to prove my sexual skills	1	2	3	4	5	6	7
10. Part of relationship responsibility	1	2	3	4	5	6	7
11. Way to have fun	1	2	3	4	5	6	7
12. Way to make up after argument or conflict	1	2	3	4	5	6	7
13. Way of exercising power and control	1	2	3	4	5	6	7
14. Way of curing boredom	1	2	3	4	5	6	7
15. Way to reduce stress	1	2	3	4	5	6	7

HOMEWORK

Handout

Based on your own life experience, prepare three messages or words of advice you would want to pass on to your son (or what you would suggest a father should pass on to his son) about how to handle sex in a meaningful relationship.

1.

2.

3.

Session 25
KIDS WHO WITNESS

MATERIALS

"Weekly Check-in"
The Great Santini (kitchen fighting scene, begin at 1:28:29, end at 1:29:57)
"When Kids See Their Parents Fight"
"Kids' Exposure to Destructive Conflicts"
"Questions for Kids"
"Kid Stories"

GOAL

To help the group members develop increased understanding of the effects of domestic violence on children and to help them develop empathy for their children.

TASKS

1. *Review "Weekly Check-in."*
2. *Review homework.*
3. *Discuss the effects of domestic violence on children.*
4. *Play* The Great Santini *(kitchen fighting scene, begin at 1:28:29, end at 1:29:57), and discuss.*
5. *Review "When Kids See Their Parents Fight."*
6. *Review "Kids Exposure to Destructive Conflicts."*
7. *Review and role-play "Questions for Kids."*
8. *Explain "Kid Stories."*
9. *Assign homework.*

PROGRAM

1. Discuss the effects on kids of witnessing domestic violence. Begin by explaining that abusive fighting—verbal and physical—affects not only the adults, but also the children who witness it. Emphasize that children usually have excellent radar for tuning in to this behavior, even if the parents are sure it is all happening behind closed doors.

181

2. Play *The Great Santini* (kitchen fighting scene, begin at 1:28:29, end at 1:29:57) and discuss. Review the ways in which each child has his or her own specific reaction to the violence. Identify self-talk for the children and the parents.

3. Review "When Kids See Their Parents Fight" and "Kids' Exposure to Destructive Conflicts." Ask the group members to identify any of these symptoms they have noticed in their own kids. Also ask them to recall experiences when they were growing up and witnessed violence between their parents.

4. Review "Questions for Kids." **This is the most important component of this session.** Select several group members, who have children who have witnessed abusive behavior in this family, to role-play this child. As this child, the man answers these questions, asked in detail by the group leaders and group members. Review the self-talk and emotions. It is often helpful to have the "kids" talk to each other about what it has been like for them.

WHEN KIDS SEE THEIR PARENTS FIGHT

 Handout

Kids will often display symptoms like these, without always being able to tell you what is bothering them:

- **Sleep problems:** fears of going to sleep; nightmares; dreams of danger

- **Mysterious aches and pains:** headaches; stomachaches, medical problems such as asthma, arthritis, ulcers

- **Fears:** anxiety about being hurt or killed; fears of going to school or of separating from mother; worrying; difficulties concentrating and paying attention

- **Behavior problems:** abusing drugs or alcohol; suicide attempts or engaging in dangerous behavior; eating problems; bed-wetting or regression to earlier developmental stages; acting perfect; overachieving; behaving like small adults

- **People problems:** losing interest in people; fighting or abusing others; outbursts of temper, tantrums

- **Emotional problems:** losing interest in activities; feeling lonely

KIDS' EXPOSURE TO DESTRUCTIVE CONFLICTS

Handout

Kids usually know what is happening when their parents are fighting. Studies indicate that kids are very aware of the level of domestic violence in the house. Most kids report that they witnessed (heard or saw) their parents fighting, even when a vast majority of the parents insisted that the kids didn't know what was going on.

Exposure to fighting makes kids more sensitive. Although it is commonly believed that kids who are exposed to parents' fighting "get used to it," studies actually indicate that they become more sensitive with exposure. As we might expect from posttraumatic stress disorder (PTSD), kids from violent homes become more rather than less upset when they are exposed to adults in conflict.

CERTAIN FACTORS SEEM TO MAKE KIDS' REACTIONS WORSE

- *Conflict-related factors:* The more intense and nasty the conflict, the more severe the kids' symptoms are likely to be.
- *Topic: "Are they arguing about me?"* If the child perceives that the argument is about him or her, the symptoms are usually worse.
- *Resolution:* Are the adults able to resolve the conflict? If that child observes that the adults are able to calm down and recover, his or her symptoms are usually reduced. There is a little less chaos and a little less to be frightened of.
- *Child involvement:* The more actively involved the child is in trying to intervene or break up the conflict, the more severe the symptoms.
- *Child's age:* The younger the child, the more likelihood there is for self-blame and for believing that "*This must be about me.*"
- *Gender of child:* Boys are more likely to blame themselves.

Future relationship behavior is affected. Boys who observe domestic violence are six times more likely to commit similar acts as an adult; girls who witness such behavior are much more likely to become abusive themselves, or to find themselves an abusive partner.

The good news is that not all kids are so negatively affected by witnessing adults in destructive conflicts. The better the relationship between child and adult, and the greater capacity to talk honestly about the child's feelings about what has happened, serves as a buffer to some of these effects. Thus, for reasons that we cannot quite explain, some kids are simply constitutionally more adaptive to bad situations.

QUESTIONS FOR KIDS*

Handout

In this exercise, group members take turns role-playing, being the child in their house who has witnessed violence. Other group members interview these "kids" about their experiences.

1. What kinds of things do your mom and dad fight about?

2. What happens when your mom or dad gets angry or your parents fight? Can you describe any fights between your parents that you saw yourself? What did you see or hear during the fight? What was it like for you afterwards (e.g., did you see your parents' injuries or the house torn apart)? What were your reactions?

3. What do you do if your parents push, shove, or hit each other? Do you leave the room or go outside?

4. Can you describe any fights between your parents in which you were caught in the middle, or when you tried to stop them? What happened?

5. Do they ever fight about you? How does this make you feel (scared, confused, sad, mad)?

6. Do you talk to anybody about this?

7. How have you handled your feelings since this has happened? Do you ever feel like hurting yourself or anyone else?

8. In an emergency for you or your parents, who would you call? Where could you go?

---

*Adapted with permission from the Family Violence Prevention Fund's publication entitled *Domestic Violence: A National Curriculum for Family Preservation Practitioners,* Schechter & Ganley (1995), p. 176. May not be reproduced without permission.

KID STORIES*

 Handout

1. **You are an 8-year-old boy**, and you really like playing video games more than anything else. Your dad has been getting drunk lately. He comes home and hits your mom, and he breaks things after he thinks the kids have gone to sleep. Your older sister has started using drugs and running away. One day after school, your mom tells you you're all going to be moving away from your dad, with her, to another town across the state, near your aunt and uncle. Your mom tells you that she can't trust your dad anymore and that you kids might be the next to get hurt. You've never seen your dad hit your sister, and he's never hit you.

    - How would you feel when you heard about your mom's plans?

    - How would you feel toward your mother?

    - How would you feel toward your father?

2. **You are a 10-year-old girl** who's been really screwing up at school lately. Your dad is constantly on your case; it seems like nothing you do is right. You know your mom has been spending a lot of money, and he is always yelling at her about it. One time he locked her out of the house, and she had to stay outside in the rain until you snuck around the back to let her in. She yells right back at him, calling him bad names. Sometimes she even throws things at him and you can hear things breaking. You and your mom have left a couple of times for a few days, but she always comes back. It's hard for you to sleep. You want this to stop, and you ask if you can live with somebody else for a while.

    - How would you feel toward your mother?

    - How would you feel toward your father?

*Adapted with permission from the Family Violence Prevention Fund's publication entitled *Domestic Violence: A National Curriculum for Family Preservation Practitioners,* Schechter & Ganley (1995), pp. 178–179. May not be reproduced without permission.

HOMEWORK

 **Handout**

Complete the "Kid Stories" handout and bring it for group review next session.

Session 26
KID STRATEGIES AND TOOLS

MATERIALS

"Weekly Check-in"
"Listening to Kids"
"Tips for Parents"
"The Right Move"

GOALS

To help group members identify their own attitudes and approaches toward their children and develop new skills in communication and problem solving.

TASKS

1. Review *"Weekly Check-in."*
2. Review homework.
3. Review *"Listening to Kids."*
4. Review *"Tips for Parents."*
5. Review *"The Right Move."*
6. Assign homework.

PROGRAM

1. Introduce the topic of parenting. Ask each of the men the name, age, and gender of each of their children and write them on the board.

2. Review "Listening to Kids." Use this handout to stimulate discussion about the self-talk, needs, and feelings that kids have. Remind the group members of their skills in active listening. Role-play different "shut down" and "open up" responses and examine the internal reactions of the kids in this dialogue.

3. Review "Tips for Parents." Discuss each of these guidelines.

4. Review "The Right Move." This section is most likely to stir up controversy as the men declare their views on discipline, punishment, spanking, and talking back. It is important to remain respectful of their points of view while still presenting new models for handling problems. Don't make the mistake of implying that this "right" approach to consequences or any other skills in parenting that we propose can serve as "magic." Any group members with kids will know that there is no such thing.

As part of a review of self-talk patterns, help the group members examine their own reasons for reacting to their kids in certain ways. Discuss the differences in motivation between wanting to punish for doing something wrong and offering consequences with the goal of correction. Which of the following might apply?

- *"I want to make it clear who's in charge."*
- *"I want to open up communication between me and my daughter or son."*
- *"It's time to express my feelings."*
- *"Nobody should be allowed to treat me like this."*
- *"I want to model positive behaviors for my kids."*
- *"I want us to solve this problem together."*
- *"I'm afraid of losing this kid."*

LISTENING TO KIDS

Handout

If you want to open up communication with kids, you need to read between the lines of what they say. Your response needs to open things up, not shut them down. As you review this list, it is important to remember the principles of active listening.

Child says:	"Shut down" Response	"Open up" Response
I'm never going to play with her again.	*Why don't you just forget it?*	*Wow! You must be really mad at that girl!*
I can't do it!	*Now, don't talk like that! You're such a quitter!*	*This really feels hard to you, doesn't it?*
I want to go, too. She always gets to go and I never do!	*We've discussed this before. Now stop fussing!*	*I know this seems really unfair to you.*
Look at this new model I put together!	*OK, that's nice. But I've got a lot of stuff to do.*	*Wow, you should feel really proud of this!*
I don't want to go to school. School is stupid!	*Everyone has to go to school! It's the law!*	*Are you worried about getting picked on again?*

For each remark, give an example of a "shut down" and an "open up":

1. *"I don't like vegetables, and I'm not going to eat them."*

2. *"Football is such a stupid game. Just write me an excuse so I can get out of it."*

3. *"I don't want to go to bed. Everyone else gets to stay up later. It's too early."*

4. *"Those shoes you bought me are so lame. There's no way I can go to school in them."*

TIPS FOR PARENTS

 Handout

Make the time: In today's complex world, it's more important than ever to set aside time to talk. That doesn't mean you have to hold a formal meeting. Sometimes the best discussions take place while you're driving the car or puttering around the kitchen.

Listen to the little stuff: Kids will talk to you if they know you're going to listen, whether they discuss heavy issues such as sex and drugs or everyday things like what happened in school. If your kids know you're listening, they're more likely to trust you enough to talk about everything in their lives.

Listen between the lines: Because a lot of kids find it hard to talk to their parents about things that really matter, parents have to pay special attention to what their kids are trying to say. It helps to pay particular attention to emotions—not just the emotion itself, but its intensity, too.

Ask their opinion: Few things please children (or anybody else) more than being asked their opinion. You don't have to ask about important issues all the time, either.

Don't interrupt: Kids say that when they talk, their parents often or sometimes don't give them a chance to explain themselves. It's a good idea to give your children some extra time to explain their opinion or desires, even if you think you know what they're going to say.

THE RIGHT MOVE

Handout

Below is a list of possible responses to some of the difficult issues that kids present to you. You should know all of these, so you have plenty to choose from when the need arises. None of these is right all the time. Sometimes they are best used in combination with other responses. Review this list to make sure you understand each item.

Active listening: Try to let your child know that you understand something about how he or she feels:

"Hey, it sounds like you are really feeling frustrated with all this."

Natural consequences: Let natural events serve as a teacher for your child, so you don't have to do anything:

"Your daughter is mean to her friends, and they stop calling her."
"Your son eats too much candy and gets a stomachache."

Logical consequences: When the parent applies consequences that fit the crime:

If the child has bad grades because he spends too much time on XBox, the XBox is restricted.
The teenager comes home drunk, so he loses driving privileges.
The child starts fight with a sibling, so he goes into time-out.

Applied consequences: When the parent has no choice but to apply consequences that don't directly make sense for the crime:

The child is rude, so TV privileges are taken away.

"I" messages: Explain to the child how you feel without applying any specific behavioral consequence:

"I really feel disappointed in you when you behave like that at Grandma's house. I know you can do better than that."

Restructuring the environment: Recognize that kids will be kids and try to arrange the situation so they are less likely to do something wrong:

Make sure that your kids have a nap before they go out to a family dinner.
Keep alcohol locked up or out of the house completely so teenagers will not have access.

As you go through the examples below, consider the different possible responses from the list above. In the group discussion, discuss the examples and the suggested responses, then come up with your own for homework. Remember that there is no one correct answer, and that several may be used in combination. You may also come up with some good ideas that are not on this list.

Child's behavior	Best response?
Teenager borrows father's tools and doesn't return them.	"I" messages Logical consequences
Child is upset about failing test at school.	Active listening Explore alternatives
Child doesn't spend any time doing her homework.	Logical consequences Natural consequences
Toddler puts finger in light socket.	Restructuring the environment
Child forgets to put bicycle away at night.	????
Teenager leaves big mess in family room.	????
Toddler throws food from his high chair.	????

HOMEWORK

 **Handout**

Fill in the blank sections from "The Right Move" handout.

PART V
STANDARD FORMS

EVALUATION FORM

This form is to be completed at the end of the group member's 13th, 26th, 39th, and 52nd sessions, as well as any other time when there are special recommendations or concerns.

Group Member's Name: _____

Group Leaders' Names: _____

Group Attended: _____ Dates: _____ to _____

Total # sessions attended: _____ Date of report: _____

Please evaluate the group member on all the scales listed below. The norm group should be the overall population of group members at this stage of treatment. Give a "1" for the lowest score on each item and a "9" for the highest score, with any number in between which best describes your assessment.

PARTICIPATION

No personal self-disclosure	1	2	3	4	5	6	7	8	9	Appropriate self-disclosure
Defensive	1	2	3	4	5	6	7	8	9	Very open to feedback
Feedback aggressive/destructive	1	2	3	4	5	6	7	8	9	Feedback constructive
Does not complete homework	1	2	3	4	5	6	7	8	9	Completes homework

BEHAVIOR

Poor ability expressing feelings	1	2	3	4	5	6	7	8	9	Excellent ability
Does not recognize responsibility for family violence	1	2	3	4	5	6	7	8	9	Recognizes responsibility
Poor control over impulses and behavior	1	2	3	4	5	6	7	8	9	Good control
Minimal empathy/concern for victim or other family members	1	2	3	4	5	6	7	8	9	Excellent empathy/concern
Little self-awareness of buildup of tension or emotional needs	1	2	3	4	5	6	7	8	9	Excellent self-awareness
Poor assertive expression of needs and feelings	1	2	3	4	5	6	7	8	9	Excellent assertiveness

Please rate the group member's overall progress, **as compared to the overall population of group members at this stage of treatment.** Rate on a scale of 1 to 9, with 1 as no improvement and 9 as outstanding improvement.

1   2   3   4   5   6   7   8   9   N/A

At this time, check the box if you recommend either of the following:

Probation _____
Termination from program _____

COMMENTS

_____

_____

_____

_____

_____

Group leader signature _____

Group leader signature _____

WEEKLY CHECK-IN

 Handout

Name: _____   Date: _____

1. **Success.** Describe one way in the past week in which you successfully kept yourself from being aggressive or successfully used something you learned in group. The success can be large or small. This is a chance to "pat yourself on the back."

   What was the situation?

   What might you have done in the past?

   What did you do right?

Calmly stood up for my rights	Told myself to relax	Took a time-out
Expressed my feelings responsibly	Changed my self-talk	Other

2. **Problem Situation.** Describe one way in the past week in which you did not handle an interpersonal situation well.

   What was the situation?

   How upset did you feel?

Not At All Upset					Upset				Extremely Upset	
1	10	20	30	40	50	60	70	80	90	100

   How did you respond?

3. **Aggression.** Did you become verbally or physically aggressive toward anyone in the past week (including threats and damage to property)?

Slapping	Kicking	Grabbing/restraining
Punching/hitting	Throwing things	Sexual abuse
Verbal/emotional abuse	Destruction of property	Kicking
	Other	

   What would you do in a similar situation in the future to avoid becoming aggressive?

4. Did you complete homework for the week?   Yes_____No_____None Assigned_____

WHAT IS MOST HELPFUL?

Handout

When asked *"What was most helpful to you in the group?,"* group members reported the items below. We want you to know the ways that "successful" group members end up feeling based on this program.

> Being able to say what was bothering me instead of holding it in.
> Learning from the group about the type of impression I make on others.
> Learning that I must take ultimate responsibility for the way I live my life no matter what others have done.
> Learning that it's OK to reveal personal things and take risks.
> Feeling more trustful of groups other people.

Below, feel free to share what was most helpful to you from this program.

GUT CHECK QUESTIONNAIRE*

Handout

Name: _____   Date: _____

Answer each of these questions as honestly as you can. None of these answers will be shared with the group without your consent. Use a number from 1 to 10, with 1 being lowest and 10 being highest. When answering questions 4, 5, and 6, remember that the purpose of this is simply to offer some valuable feedback to one of your peers. Most of us have trouble seeing ourselves without honest feedback from others who care about us.

1. How honest am I being in the group? *(not at all/completely)* _____ (1–10)

2. How much effort am I putting into the group? *(none/very much)* _____ (1–10)

3. How much feedback am I giving to others in the group? *(none/very much)* _____ (1–10)

4. Who do I know the most/least in the group?

   Most _____

   Least _____

5. Who is acknowledging responsibility for his relationship problems most in the group?

   Most _____

6. Who is being the most emotionally honest in the group?

   Most _____

7. How much am I getting out of the group?

   Nothing   A lot

   1   2   3   4   5   6   7   8   9   10

*Adapted from Dutton (1998), p. 171–72.

REFERENCES

Amherst H. Wilder Foundation (1995). *Foundations for violence-free living: A step-by-step guide to facilitating men's domestic abuse groups.* St. Paul, MN: Author.

Browne, K., Saunders, D., & Staecker, K. (1997). Process-psychodynamic groups for men who batter: A brief treatment model. *Families in Society: The Journal of Contemporary Human Services,* 265–271.

Dutton, D. (1998). *The abusive personality: Violence and control in intimate relationships.* New York: Guilford Press.

Dutton, D., with Golant, S. (1995). *The batterer: A psychological profile.* New York: Basic Books.

Dutton, D., van Ginkel, C., & Strazomski, A. (1995). The role of shame and guilt in the intergenerational transmission of abusiveness. *Violence and Victims, 10*(2), 121–131.

Erickson, M. & Rossi, E. (1979). *Hypnotherapy: An exploratory casebook.* New York: Irvington Publishers.

Fischer, G. (1986). College student attitudes toward forcible date rape. *Journal of Sex Education and Therapy, 12,* 42–46.

Geffner, R., & Mantooth, C. (1995). *A psychoeducational model for ending wife/partner abuse: A program manual for treating individuals and couples.* Tyler, TX: Family Violence and Sexual Assault Institute.

Gilligan, S. (1987). *Therapeutic trances.* New York: Brunner Mazel.

Gottman, J. (1994). *Why marriages succeed and fail.* New York: Simon & Schuster.

Gottman, J. (1999). *The marriage clinic.* New York: W. W. Norton.

Gottman, J. (2000). The seven principles for making marriage work. New York: Three Rivers Press.

Gottman, J., Coan, J., Carrere, S., & Swanson, C. (1998). Predicting marital happiness and stability from newlywed interactions. *Journal of Marriage and the Family, 60,* 5–22.

Gottman, J., Jacobson, J., Rushe, R., Short, J., Babcock, J., La Taillade, J., & Waltz, J. (1995). The relationship between heart rate activity, emotionally aggressive behavior, and general violence in batterers. *Journal of Family Psychology, 9,* 227–248.

Hare, R. (1993). *Without conscience.* New York: Pocket Books.

Harway, M., & Evans, K. (1996). Working in groups with men who batter. In M. Andronico (Ed.), *Men in groups: Insights, interventions, and psychoeducational work* (pp. 357–375). Washington, DC: American Psychological Association.

Henry, W., Schacht, T., & Strupp, H. (1986). Structural analysis of social behavior: Application to a study of interpersonal process in differential psychotherapeutic outcome. *Journal of Consulting and Clinical Psychology, 54,* 27–31.

Henry, W, Schacht, T., & Strupp, H. (1990). Patient and therapist introject, interpersonal process, and differential psychotherapy outcome. *Journal of Consulting and Clinical Psychology, 58,* 768–774.

Holtzworth-Munroe, A. & Hutchinson, G. (1993). Attributing negative intent to wife behavior: The attributions of maritally violent versus nonviolent men. *Journal of Abnormal Psychology, 102*(2), 206–211.

Holtzworth-Munroe, A., Meehan, J., Herron, K., Rehman, U., & Stuart, G. (2000). Testing the Holtzworth-Munroe and Stuart (1994) Batterer Typology. *Journal of Consulting and Clinical Psychology, 68*(6), 1000–1019.

Holtzworth-Munroe, A., & Stuart, G. (1994). Typologies of male batterers: Three subtypes and the differences among them. *Psychological Bulletin, 116*, 476–497.

Hotaling, G., & Sugarman, D. (1986). An analysis of risk markers in husband to wife violence: The current state of knowledge. *Violence and Victims, 1*, 101–124.

Jacobson, N. & Gottman, J. (1998a, March/April). Anatomy of a violent relationship. *Psychology Today*, 60–84.

Jacobson, N., & Gottman, J. (1998b). *When men batter women*. New York: Simon & Schuster.

Johnson, M. (1995). Patriarchal terrorism and common couple violence: Two forms of violence against women. *Journal of Marriage and the Family, 57*, 283–294.

Kalmuss, D. (1984). The intergenerational transmission of marital aggression. *Journal of Marriage and the Family, 46*, 11–19.

Lee, M., Greene, G., Uken, A., Rheinscheld, L., & Sebold, J. (1997). *Solution-focused brief treatment: A viable modality for treating domestic violence offenders?* Paper presented at the 5th International Family Violence Research Conference, Durham, NH, June 29–July 2.

Millon, T., Millon, C., Davis, R., & Grossman, S. (2006). *Millon Clinical Multiaxial Inventory—III*. Minneapolis, MN: Pearson Assessments.

Murphy, C., & Baxter, V. (1997). Motivating batterers to change in the treatment context. *Journal of Interpersonal Violence, 12*(4), 607–619.

O'Hanlon, W., & Weiner-Davis, M. (1989). *In search of solutions*. New York: W. W. Norton.

Pence, E., & Paymar, M. (1993). *Education groups for men who batter: The Duluth model*. New York: Springer.

Pleck, J. (1980). Men's power with women, other men, and society. In E. Pleck & J. Pleck (Eds.), *The American man* (pp. 417–433). Englewood Cliffs, NJ: Prentice-Hall.

Prince, J., & Arias, I. (1994). The role of perceived control and the desirability of control among abusive and nonabusive husbands. *American Journal of Family Therapy, 22*(2), 126–134.

Schechter, S., & Ganley, A. L. (1995). *Domestic violence: A national curriculum for family preservation practitioners*. San Francisco: Family Violence Prevention Fund.

Shapiro, S. (1995). *Talking with patients: A self psychological view*. Northvale, NJ: Jason Aronson.

Stosny, S. (1995). *Treating attachment abuse: A compassionate approach*. New York: Springer.

Stosny, S. (2001). Personal communication.

Straus, M., Gelles, R., & Steinmetz, S. (1980). *Behind closed doors: Violence in the American family*. Garden City, NY: Doubleday.

Wachter, O., & Boyd T. (1982). Time out. In M. Roy (Ed.), *The abusive partner: An analysis of domestic battering* (pp. 265–266). New York: Van Nostrand Reinhold.

Walker, L. (1984). *The battered woman syndrome*. New York: Springer.

Weiss, J., & Sampson, H. (1986). *The psychoanalytic process*. New York: Guilford Press.

Wexler, D. (1991a). *The adolescent self: Strategies for self-management, self-soothing, and self-esteem in adolescence*. New York: W. W. Norton.

Wexler, D. (1991b). *The PRISM workbook*. New York: W. W. Norton.

Wexler, D. (1999). The broken mirror: A self psychological treatment perspective for relationship violence. *Journal of Psychotherapy Practice and Research, 8*(2), 129–141.

Wexler, D. (2000). *Domestic violence 2000: An integrated skills program for men*. New York: W. W. Norton.

Wexler, D. (2004). *When good men behave badly: Change your behavior, change your relationship*. Oakland, CA: New Harbinger.

White, M., & Weiner, M. (1986). *The theory and practice of self psychology*. New York: Brunner Mazel.

Wolf, E. (1988). *Treating the self: Elements of clinical self psychology*. New York: Guilford Press.

Wolfe, B. (1989). Heinz Kohut's self psychology: A conceptual analysis. *Psychotherapy, 26,* 545–554.

Yalom, I. (1995). *The theory and practice of group psychotherapy* (3rd ed.). New York: Basic Books.

INDEX

Page numbers followed by an "*n*" indicate a footnote.